BEATRICE WEBB

Portrait of a Reformist

Dr Thamizhachi Thangapandian

Vitasta

Published by
Renu Kaul Verma
Vitasta Publishing Pvt Ltd
4348/4C, Ansari Road, Daryaganj
New Delhi - 110 002
info@vitastapublishing.com

ISBN: 978-81-19670-83-3

First Edition 2025
MRP ₹495

Edited by Abhijit Baroi
Layout & Cover Design by Rohit Gautam
Printed by Chaman Enterprises, New Delhi

Contents

Dedication *v*
Acknowledgements *vii*
Foreword *ix*
Preface *xiii*
Introduction *xxi*

Webb's Criticism of Her Class 1
Portrait of an Ethos 21
Webb's Interest in the Working Class 39
My Apprenticeship as an Autobiography 55
A Fascinating Moment in Social History 66

Notes *73*
Bibliography *77*
Author Bio *79*

To

Prof T V Subba Rao,
my mentor and an incomparable guide
who has left an indelible mark on me with his
great legacy as a phenomenal teacher
&
Prof Paul Sharrad,
Independent Scholar, Fellow,
University of Wollongong, NSW, Australia,
for always encouraging me in my pursuit of
research, with his unstinted
support and warmth.

Acknowledgements

If you work in a field of inquiry, say a thesis, you are bound to wonder where its good ideas come from. I got my own from Professor T V Subba Rao (Retd) of Andhra Pradesh Open University, who brought about in me an awareness about an extraordinary woman as well as a remarkable literary figure, Beatrice Webb, who put the best version of herself into her autobiography entitled *My Apprenticeship*. I am sure that, for developing conceptual maturity in my topic, I was guided more by Professor Subba Rao's classic method of sifting works and assessing their value than anything else. This is a small acknowledgement, considering how he helped me in making the right choices and how he trained me to put my learning to good use for this entire work.

I would also like to thank Professor Shakthivelan, my guide and the Head of the Department of English, Thiagarajar College of Arts & Science, Madurai, for offering worthy suggestions and revising my work.

I am particularly indebted to Dr Padmanaban, Professor of English, Thiagarajar College of Arts & Science, Madurai, for his laborious assistance and my many significant discussions with him, both of which helped me complete my work satisfactorily.

I also thank Dr Raja Govindasamy, Professor of English, Thiagarajar College of Arts & Science, Madurai, for his kind assistance by way of providing me the necessary books for my dissertation.

For the other source materials, I am beholden to the British Council Library, Chennai.

***

Foreword

One of the delights of working in the humanities is the serendipitous connection that reveals something of direct interest by disparate routes. In this case, an Australian learns his own political history through encountering a book about an English woman written by an Indian scholar. Dr Sumathy's study of the English activist Beatrice Webb leads me to discover that Australia's historian Manning Clark and its reformist Prime Minister Gough Whitlam were both influenced by Webb's Fabian socialism. (Fitzgerald).

Not a lot has been written about Webb as a literary figure. Other than brief biographies, articles concentrate on the Webbs' travels, on Beatrice's connections with Bernard Shaw and Virginia Woolf, and on the conundrum of radical women opposing the suffragette movement. Webb's story presents an interesting set of contradictions: a well-off person mixing with and advocating for the poor; a conservative upholder of gender roles and the sanctity of marriage (like South African Olive Schreiner and South Australian Catherine Helen Spence) preaching the value of women's work. The author here investigates some of these complexities with a focus on Webb's memoir, *My Apprenticeship*.

The study began as an M Phil thesis some time ago and since then, there has been a boom in studies of life writing, in particular by women. Norman MacKenzie wrote *Beatrice Webb: The Novelist Who Never Was* in 1984 and three articles have compared Webb's autobiography to other writing by such figures as Harriet Martineau (Hewett, Randall, Zwierlein). Despite this, there remains room for a book on Beatrice Webb's life and writing, and this volume brings the two together in interesting ways.

There is good reason for the author to resurrect her work of years ago. Dr Sumathy has combined her career as a poet with one promoting rational thinking and social uplift. This book on Beatrice Webb, while focusing on the literary qualities in her autobiography, is also an *homage* to the exponent of Fabian socialism that advocated peaceful permeation of democratic systems and serves as a auto-critical manifesto on the part of the scholar and politician-to-be. To paraphrase a sentence in the first chapter of the dissertation, it provided the author with a mirror of 'how her private experience could be transformed into public meaning'. As a result, the dissertation finds itself interested in the unresolved tensions in Webb's life, in particular her Victorian struggle to hold science and religion together. It is most clearly focused on the subject's discovery of a satisfactory political standpoint rather than on the literary style or psychological self-representation of the autobiography.

Chapter five gets down to literary business, appropriately locating Webb's apprenticeship narrative in a mesh of Victorian autobiographies and identifying its connection to a conversion narrative: *My Apprenticeship* follows the pattern of fall and rise manifest in 'loss of orthodox faith, a period of crisis, of acute despair and dejection', a search for something new and 'rebirth in newfound faith and vocation'. Webb's reading of St Augustine's *Confessions* is mentioned and her writing is contrasted to the more inward-looking work of Ruskin and compared to John Stuart Mill's autobiography. Webb may have deplored the apolitical evangelical faith of factory workers but she reproduces the habit of protestant self-inspection when she asks herself whether her wish to solve social problems is mere vanity. This kind of autobiographical analysis is, however, overtaken by accounts of her work, becoming more of a memoir as political *Bildung*.

I commend this study to readers, who no doubt will discover through it new connections of their own, just as I did.

Dr Paul Sharrad
Independent Scholar, Fellow
University of Wollongong, NSW, Australia

Bibliography

1. Fitzgerald, Ross. *Manning Clark and the Webbs. Quadrant.* 64.7-8 (2020) 94–95.
2. Hewitt, Martin. *Diary, Autobiography and the Practice of Life History* in Amigoni, David, ed. and intro. *Life Writing and Victorian Culture.* Routledge, 2006, 21–39, MacKenzie, Norman. *Beatrice Webb: The Novelist who Never Was Essays by Divers Hands.* 43 (1984) 104–116.
3. Nadel, Ira Bruce. *Beatrice Webb's Literary Success Studies in Short Fiction.* 13 (1976) 441–46.
4. Nord, Deborah Epstein. *Beatrice Webb and the Affirmation of Progress: The Writing of My Apprenticeship Prose Studies: History, Theory, Criticism.* 3.3 (1980) 254–70.
5. Randall, Bryony. *'Telling the Day in Beatrice Potter Webb and Dorothy Richardson: The Temporality of the Working Woman.' Modernist Cultures.* 5.2 (2010) 243–66.
6. Zwierlein, Anne-Julia. *Autobiographie und Handlungsautonomie in der ersten britischen Frauenbewegung* in Depkat, Volker and Pyta Wolfram, eds. *Autobiographie zwischen Text und Quelle.* Duncker & Humbolt, 2017, 151–65.

Preface

Deborah Epstein Nord, author of *The Apprenticeship of Beatrice Webb*, 'Leavis placed *My Apprenticeship* within a tradition of Victorian autobiography and within the context of a Victorian debate between 'Benthamite' and 'Coleridgian' attitudes. *My Apprenticeship* is important as intellectual history and as social history, but it is also 'one of the classics', Leavis asserts, because of the quality of its writing: 'we recognise in the writer a potential novelist'.

'If, as Leavis suggested, we examine Webb's memoir in the context of Victorian autobiographical literature, we can recognise it as a breakthrough in the history of women's writing rather than as an example of a woman's retreat from introspection or personal confession.

'By considering the events surrounding the writing of *My Apprenticeship*, we are able to see further that the resolutions of autobiography often mask the unresolved contradictions of life, and that Webb's memoir, though a historical record, is also a fiction.'

Professor T V Subba Rao (fondly called Prof TVS), my most cherished mentor and guide, is an iconic personality who played a pivotal role in shaping my literary preferences, refining my taste, and enhancing my creativity. I am what I am today because of him. It was he who introduced me to Beatrice Webb, upon whose contributions I submitted my MPhil dissertation, now published as a book.

After completing my graduation in English literature, I felt confident not only in my language skills, but also as a 'bluestocking', and I thought I had learnt everything about that language and its rich literature. However, when I enrolled in the postgraduate English Literature course at Thiyagarajar Arts College, Madurai, Prof Subba Rao, who profoundly influenced my intellectual journey, made me realise how amateurish I was!

He urged me to explore literature in other languages while grounding myself in my mother tongue. He encouraged me to train my mind to understand and appreciate the classics of my native language. This directive challenged me to set aside preconceived notions and forget what I thought I knew, emphasising that true education is about channelling thoughts and emotions effectively for critical appreciation and evaluation. He guided me to approach global literature with a new perspective—to observe great critical minds and creative souls with a quest to understand both oneself and the outside world. He insisted that honing our skills in the classics of our native language (our mother tongue) is the primary step before climbing the ladder of aesthetic appreciation and objective critical evaluation. He stressed that understanding the nuances of how great minds work is essential.

His most enlightening lectures in the late 1980s introduced me to the critical traditions of English literary giants like T S Eliot, Matthew Arnold, I A Richards, and F R Leavis. He exposed me to great philosophers like Kant, Hegel, Nietzsche, and Karl Marx, as well as profound literary minds such as Dostoevsky, Balzac, D H Lawrence, George Eliot, John Donne, and most importantly, John Stuart Mill, Sidney Webb, and Beatrice Webb. These introductions unveiled new dimensions to my literary understanding. Through his own life experiences, Prof Subba Rao emphasised that pursuing literature in one's mother tongue is the proudest identity. Yet, he made us scale the heights of exploring and enjoying literary works in other languages, especially English. Had he not cautioned me against the allure of false attractions that an Indian mind educated in English might encounter, I wouldn't have evolved into the *Vanapechi* that I am today.

The literary path he paved, combining a nuanced understanding of my mother tongue, an appreciation for other languages, and respect for translations, continues to influence me. His mentorship during my postgraduate college years remains invaluable, infusing freshness, resilience, taste, and a broad critical outlook into my literary pursuits. It ultimately led me to study the life of Beatrice Webb and write a dissertation on her for my Master of Philosophy.

Beatrice Webb is a remarkable woman in the history of England. She is remarkable not only as a social worker, political leader, and social critic, but also as an author of literary talent. I discuss mainly her autobiography as a literary achievement, while touching on her other roles related to my purpose. She has an original mind. Being born in a very rich family and brought up in mid-Victorian England, she became an avowed socialist by her own perceptions. She was able to rise to a true sense of her age, whereas such a sense of it, is very rare among her own distinguished contemporaries. By her efforts to learn and by her preoccupation with the interests of life she has so matured as to be free from Victorian individualism and self-regarding interests. Even as an author, there is nothing professional about her work. The great distinction she carries with her is that she worked with mature minds in the interests of the labour movement.

Beatrice Webb, remembered for her pioneering work on the co-operative movement and as the germinator of the idea of the Welfare State in the annals of Victorian England, is also a talented literary author. Her only published autobiography, *My Apprenticeship* stands testimony to her literary eloquence. Thus, the dissertation titled *Literary Merits of Beatrice Webb* with reference to her autobiography *'My Apprenticeship'* was pursued to expound the reFable bequest of Webb as a literary author.

Her autobiography, *My Apprenticeship* should be recognised as an English classic which has a special value for the reader whose interests are in the first place 'literary'.

It indicates her marvellous energy and wide range of interests. What is astonishing is her readiness to spend a decade on a research project, above all, through the 'platform' she built for herself. It is surely a living proof of Beatrice's belief that 'Society is geared to the individual'.

My Apprenticeship is a meticulous memoir interwoven with critical reflections on the politics and ideologies of the Victorian period of England. Through a web of intricate narration, Webb highlights the conditions of the working classes, nuances of class structure, and the cultural milieu pertaining to that era. The autobiography also reveals Webb's transition of a young woman into an introspective investigator and an advocate of reformed socialism.

In line with the tropes typical to the genre of autobiographies, it traces the trajectory of her life beginning from her loss of faith in traditional belief systems, her grappling with various theories of social reform and practices of social investigation of her times—a period of extensive research and field work coupled with intensive soul search for a meaning and purpose of *her* life, and finally emerging transformed with a new belief system and vocation. In her case, it led to the creation of her own version of Socialism which ultimately led to the germination and recommendation of the idea of a Welfare State and delineating her own method of social investigation in the field of social research.

Webb's autobiography details a fascinating period in the social history of Victorian England. It is the story of a young woman born in a high capitalist family with close ties to the inner circles of power in Imperial England. In it are luminaries discussing fashionable intellectual currents of the day, groping to find a solution to the pressing labour problem of the times. Born and brought up in such an era, Webb's search for a meaning and purpose for her life drifted naturally towards the living conditions of the working classes. Beginning from an inquiry to ameliorate the drastic conditions of life of the labour class, Webb laboured through the conflicting views of political and social reform, evolving her own ideas about social and political action.

This dissertation which is brought out now as a book is an analysis of Webb's autobiography, *My Apprenticeship*, laying emphasis on its literary value. It asserts the literary value by tracing her life detailed in the work as a gradual evolution and comparing it to other works of literary and intellectual merit, in particular, her contemporaries. The first chapter provides an introduction while the second chapter gives an account of how Webb could rise above her class and criticise it. The third chapter presents *My Apprenticeship* as a portrait of the Victorian age. In the fourth chapter, I have presented a study on how Webb grew to have an interest in the working class. The fifth chapter discusses the place of *My Apprenticeship* in autobiographical literature. This is followed by the sixth chapter which sums up the analysis.

I am extremely grateful to Dr Paul Sharrad (Independent Scholar and Fellow, University of Wollongong, NSW, Australia) for his unstinting support in encouraging my research journey. He has always played a significant role with his warm encouragement—whether it was evaluating my doctoral thesis, launching it when it was published as a book, or offering guidance whenever needed. I am immensely thankful for his well researched foreword to this book and for his assistance in helping me arrive at a suitable title.

I am also thankful to Vitasta Publications and its editorial team for bringing out a wonderful version of my dissertation.

As I hold this book, I cherish the legacy and memory of Prof T V Subba Rao, who is deeply missed—with immense gratitude.

Dr Thamizhachi Thangapandian
January 2025

Introduction

A major figure in the social history of England, Beatrice Webb was an acclaimed social worker, political leader and a social critic. Apart from these dimensions, Webb also proved to be an author with immense literary flair. Her autobiography heralds her literary achievement and merits elaborate discussion. Webb wrote her biography as a task; it was no more tiring than endless reading and 'hardly more so than my desperate attempt... to knit soldiers' socks.'[1] Besides the need for distraction, moreover, she had another motive for turning to this 'secret and pleasurable occupation.' She had always wanted to go back over her early life and examine how she had grown from a clever but withdrawn child into a notable social investigator and reformer—to discover, if she could, how her private experience had been transformed into public meaning. The autobiography is not only an appropriate form for such reflections, but also a branch of literature when it achieves such quality as *My Apprenticeship*.[2]

In this experiment, she found a long-desired opportunity to release her creative abilities and allow her current imagination to infuse the reality of her past. *My Apprenticeship* thus became the most distinctive thing she ever wrote. For Webb's contemporaries, it was a surprising book which revealed a very different woman from her forbidding public image. Webb herself was, in particular, delighted by a friend's comment that *My Apprenticeship* was 'the description of Victorian society'.[3] For all her misgivings, she had indeed written an unusual and remarkable book, brilliantly conceived, effectively expressed in clear prose, intellectually rigorous and yet humanly engaging.

Webb was an exceptional person, with the gift for observation, the knack of pointed comment and the habit of self-examination, all of which are indispensable attributes of the successful diarist. She cared little for the conventional purpose of the diary as a rather haphazard record of events. She often used it as a work-book in which she scribbled extracts from what she was reading, filling pages at a time with notes on religion, stubs on English history, fragments of classical philosophy or German literature. Like John Stuart Mill and John Ruskin, two other anxious and self-regarding Victorians who were also endowed with great powers of description and a feeling that they should be used for the public good, Webb turned naturally to self-explanation as a congenial means of stating the tension between the promptings of individualism and the claims of society.

In one of the most memorable sentences in *My Apprenticeship*, she wrote tellingly of 'the flight of emotion away from the service of God to the service of man.' In subduing the chaos of her feelings to the discipline of social work, she had found a compromise which might satisfy her urge to independence and appease the haunting image of her mother. As she was no philosopher, she presented her beliefs in 'the simpler form of personal experience.' She was, however, a social scientist, and *My Apprenticeship* is the autobiography not only of a Victorian and of a woman, but of a sociologist as well.

In the introduction to *My Apprenticeship*, Webb writes that beneath the surface of daily existence, her life had been determined by an opposition, 'a continuous controversy between an Ego that affirms and an Ego that denies.'[4] With this phrase, she signals an entry into the familiar world of Victorian dichotomies.

She justifies her autobiography as a sociologist's means of revealing her ideas and her identity:

> ...the very subject-matter of my science is society, its main instrument is social intercourse; thus I can hardly leave out of the picture the experience I have gathered, not deliberately as a scientific worker, but casually as a child, unmarried woman, wife and citizen. For the sociologist...is in a quite unique manner the creature of his environment. Birth and parentage, the mental atmosphere of class and creed in which he is bred, the characteristics and attainments of the men and women

> who have been his guides and associates, come first and foremost of all the raw material upon which he works.[5]

The vocation of social science, combined with the creed of socialism that constitutes her 'inevitable bias,' can best be made intelligible through an explanation of the social milieu from which she came and against which she reacted. Here, the justification of the autobiographer and the logic of the sociologist merge.

Webb's 'inevitable bias'—her eventual political and social attitudes and prejudices—evolved, at least in part, through a rejection of certain elements of what she saw as her (Potter) family's orthodoxy. She writes in her autobiography that the Potter household was dominated by the spirit of capitalist enterprise and that the family's participation in the habitual comings and goings of upper middle-class life was what Webb called a 'nomadic' existence, characterised by perpetual movement and change:

> The world of human intercourse in which I was brought up was in fact an endless series of human beings, unrelated one to the other and only casually connected with the family group—a miscellaneous crowd who came and went out of our lives, rapidly and unexpectedly. Servants came and went; governesses and tutors came and went; businessmen of all sorts... came and went; perpetually changing circles of 'London Society' acquaintances came and went...

> Our social relations had no roots in neighbourhood, in vocation, in creed, or for that matter in race; they likened a series of moving pictures—surface impressions without depth—restlessly stimulating in their glittering variety.[6]

Webb attributes to her father, Richard Potter, the ethic of amorality that she finds to be characteristic of a mid-Victorian 'capitalist at large.' He was fickle in politics and in religion. He dismissed as 'moral pedantry' conduct that was dictated by anything other than pragmatism or personal allegiance. Webb takes him to task for having no fixed principles, no fixed faith and, above all, 'no clear vision of the public good.' The constant change and movement of the Potter household and the ambition, unencumbered by ethics, of Richard Potter are understood in Dickens' vision of the effects of industrial capitalism on family life.

IF RICHARD Potter appeared chameleon-like to his daughter, Webb's mother, Laurencina Potter, appeared hidebound to strict Utilitarian politics and laissez-faire economics. Mrs Potter was raised on Adam Smith, Robert Malthus and Nassau William Senior and her closest intellectual confidante was Herbert Spencer. Mrs Potter's belief in the law of self-interest was absolute:

> It seemed to her the bounden duty of every citizen to better his social status; to ignore those beneath him and to aim steadily at the top rung of the social ladder. Only by this persistent pursuit by each individual of his own and his family's interest would the highest general level of civilisation be attained.[7]

Webb sums up her mother's philosophy of life and work in a mid-Victorian maxim: 'The man who sells his cow too cheap goes to hell.' Webb's father minimised the importance of a consistent faith and her mother's social philosophy was at odds with what she understood to be a truly Christian spirit.

In Webb's life, Herbert Spencer played the unique role of the first intellectual mentor:

> It was the philosopher on the hearth who, alone among my elders...encouraged me in my lonely studies; who heard patiently and criticised kindly my untutored scribblings about Greek and German philosophers.[8]

From him she first learned to regard social institutions, as 'organisms' to be observed and explained, to understand the usefulness of facts—'a gift said to be rare in a woman and of untold importance to the social investigator.' Even more important was the example of continuous concentrated effort in carrying out, with a heroic disregard of material prosperity and physical comfort, a task which he believed would further human progress. Webb notes, in comparing the influences on her of Herbert Spencer and Martha Jackson, that he was 'in intellect towering above her, but in emotional insight depths below her.' She herein identifies one of the dichotomies that dominated her own life: the debate, familiar to so many Victorian autobiographers, between intellect and emotion; between reason and feeling.

The most far-reaching and influential of Martha's gifts was her revelation of the meaning of the religious spirit. The first reflections of Webb debating Egos are visible in her connections to these two early mentors, one spiritual and the other intellectual. Spencer convinced her that a science of society was indeed possible and, at the same time, caused her to question the adequacy of science in solving social problems.

Martha Jackson alerted her to the need for 'religion as well as science, emotional faith as well as intellectual curiosity.' And Laurencina Potter's political and economic orthodoxies, combined with a personal coldness and aloofness, served ultimately to alienate her daughter from a rigid utilitarian point of view and from a way of dealing with people according to the rules of political economy.

Living in what she called a stronghold of capitalism, surrounded by the pleasure-grounds of London, she distrusted the adulation of personality and the influence of worldly experience. She does record in the autobiography, in words recalling both Mill's and Carlyle's rejection of the goal of happiness, 'a new-found determination to begin to live for others and take what happiness comes to us by the way.' The path of personal happiness and gratification having been blocked, she decided to make service and work her goals.

The Victorian notion of vocation of faith, coupled with work for the good of humanity, evolved in her consciousness as she emerged from her silent agony of 1885–86. She was now aware of having a special mission to the society at large and of being but an instrument to be handled, or thrown on one side, by a Greater Power. Like Wordsworth, she felt herself to be among the elect and, like Carlyle and Mill, she found work for the common good to be the cure for 'despairing self-consciousness.'

During these 'years of apprenticeship,' when faith and work set the tone of her daily life, Webb discovered her vocation and, in so doing, began the gradual conversion to socialism that is the central theme of *My Apprenticeship*. This conversion, from individualism to collectivism, had its roots in her rejection of the ethos of her home and was set in motion when she took up the craft of social investigation. The faith toward which she gravitated was generated out of the work she did in the 1880s and out of the political temper of the decade. Her crisis of the 1880s ended in a commitment to the work of social investigation and a translation of the remnants of her Christian faith into the 'faith' of socialism.

If science was to be the method and service the purpose, Webb drew the inference that the most hopeful form of social service was the craft of a social investigator. 'What roused and absorbed my curiosity,' she writes, 'were men and women, regarded—if I may use an old-fashioned word—as 'souls,' their past and present conditions of life, their thoughts and feelings and their constantly changing behavior.' The union of a glorification of science with a 'religion of humanity' suited Victorian intellectual needs and made the 'science of society' appear a logical and morally justified vocation.

The craft of social investigation, sanctioned by the ethos of the 1880s and by the philosophies of men such as Comte, was not yet recognised in the laboratories of the universities and Webb's apprenticeship took place in the field and at her own desk, at first under her own supervision and ultimately under the direction of one of the first of English scientific social investigators, Charles Booth.

As Webb went from one project to another, rejecting certain established kinds of work and inventing new ones, she moved closer and closer to a rejection of individualism and to an acceptance of collectivism. Like Mark Rutherford, who discovered a new form of faith only after he had found vocation, Webb was brought to the 'creed' of Fabianism only after she had made social investigation her 'craft.'

Even as an author, there is nothing professional about her work. The great distinction she carries with her is that she worked with mature minds in the interests of the labour movement. An account of this work is what is essential for placing her. Her autobiography indicates her marvellous energy and wide range of interests.

In a series of letters to her father, woven into the text of

My Apprenticeship, Webb described the working, religious and social life of the Bacup factory workers and artisans. She felt personally comforted and warmed by the spirit of religion and community she observed. She also wrote about her fears for the future of the community if religious faith should lose its hold. Webb was anxious to explore solutions to the problems of poverty, unemployment, social and economic inequities and the oppressive conditions of work; so she left the study of London poverty and set out, in the year 1889, to begin a study of the history of the co-operative movement in Britain.

If the primary theme of *My Apprenticeship* is Webb's quest for 'creed' and 'craft' through a working out of the conflict between the 'Ego that affirms' and the 'Ego that denies,' its secondary theme is the resolution of that other division of self she experienced as an intellectually ambitious Victorian woman. Growing up in an age that clearly separated the spheres of men and women, she found it all but impossible to reconcile her longings for public achievement with her desire for the private happiness of marriage and domesticity. Like Margaret Fuller, she aspired to some integration, some 'union,' of the two beings who seemed to co-exist uncomfortably within her. Like so many other accomplished Victorian women, she could not understand the two seemingly irreconcilable impulses.

My Apprenticeship shares this theme of division with memories of other nineteenth-century women and with some of the major works of fiction by Victorian women novelists and, in its way, it represents an amalgam of two genres of women's writing. Like a memoir, it is the factual record of a life; however, like a work of fiction, it also achieves what other memoirs by nineteenth-century women did not: A structural and thematic coherence through the explicit exposition and resolution of conflicts unique to the women of her age, *My Apprenticeship* is surely a living proof of Webb's belief that 'society is geared to the individual.'

Webb thought she might not find her usefulness as a woman in marriage and maternity, but she would surely find it in a life combining faith and work, in a life of service. She had written to her father from the East End, just before he became ill, that the strong women she met working there had a great future before them in the solution of social questions. '(Though) they may have masculine faculty, but they have the woman's temperament and the stronger they are the most distinctively feminine they are.'

Webb now saw herself as one of these women, able to combine a woman's temperament and a woman's faith with a 'masculine faculty in the service of humanity.' The addition of faith to her determination to work at a craft also served to eliminate from her ambitions the 'vanity motive,' which had been so disquieting to Webb in the days before she met Chamberlain. The idea of service, of working for the good of others in the spirit of religious faith, seemed to her to solve the problem of egoism. She continued to wonder, in the pages of her diary, if her desire to devote her life to the solving of social questions was presumptuous and vain. She fought the moments in which she fell prey to 'passion, self-consciousness and egoism' and prayed that her life might be a useful one, that she might 'dedicate (herself) earnestly and without trembling to a search after the truths' that would help other people. Marriage to Sidney Webb was to be but a continuation of this mission: a way of preserving aspirations and commitments to a public role.

My Apprenticeship belongs to the tradition of Victorian autobiography because of the nature of its content—it places the phenomenon of conversion at its centre, traces the dialectic between faith and reason and treats the discovery of vocation as the essential moment of individual life. *My Apprenticeship* belongs to the tradition of women's writing because it focuses on the resolution of female conflict and on the problematic reconciliation of the private and public spheres. Political events, economic crises and intellectual movements from the subjects of *My Apprenticeship* describe Webb's professional and political evolution in the decade of the 1880s.

The progress Webb found lacking in the evolution of society might have been present in her personal history. If society had not been moving towards wholeness, perhaps she had been doing so in her own life. Her faith might have been redeemed by a discovery of private meaning. The history of mankind did not now seem to her a 'connected whole,' as Herbert Spencer had taught her and as she and Sidney had so fervently believed; but the writing of her autobiography might prove that design and purpose could be detected at least in the individual life. The writing of My Apprenticeship was, then, Webb's response to the public and personal crisis of the First World War.

The process of writing *My Apprenticeship* satisfied her need to create something of her own. In this book, Webb chose an autobiographical form that gave intellectual and spiritual debate a central role, a place of prominence. In a discussion of *My Apprenticeship*, Patricia Meyer Spacks recognises Webb's 'case history' as 'paradigmatic of a woman suspended between the categories of feeling and reason, love and work, 'feminine' emotion and masculine intellect. Spacks appreciates the examination of these dichotomies in the beginning section of *My Apprenticeship*, but she regrets Webb's early abandonment of the subject of female conflict for the subject of works: 'More and more, her autobiography begins to record her work rather than her life.'[9]

The enthusiasm of reviewers and friends for Webb's *My Apprenticeship* and their recognition of its value as a clue to her identity, ultimately prompted critics of literature to take the book seriously and thereby, contribute indirectly to the revision of Webb's image in history.

F R Leavis suggested, in an introduction to John Stuart Mill's essays on Bentham and Coleridge, that *My Apprenticeship* ought to be read not merely as 'the life's record of a notability' but as one of the classics of English literature;[10] that Webb's autobiography belonged in a discussion of Mill's seminal essays because, in its 'classically representative way, it described, as did Mill's own autobiography,' 'a most important part of the intellectual history of the nineteenth century.'[11]

Leavis placed *My Apprenticeship* within a tradition of Victorian autobiography and within the context of a Victorian debate and 'Benthamite' and 'Coleridgean' attitudes. '*My Apprenticeship* is important as intellectual history and as social history, but it is also one of the classics,' Leavis asserts, because of the quality of its writing: 'We recognise in the writer a potential novelist.'

Webb reminds Leavis of George Eliot, not just because both were 'gifted and highly intellectual women' and both closely connected to Herbert Spencer, but also because they were similarly 'earnest, strong in sympathetic imagination and religiously given beneath all the liberal convictions of... intellect.'[12] Webb, like Eliot, had a 'novelist's interest in the concrete... (and) in the individual life.'[13] If, as Leavis suggested, we examine Webb's memoir in the context of Victorian autobiographical literature, we can recognise it as a breakthrough in the history of women's writing rather than as an example of a woman's retreat from introspection or personal confession.

The process of writing *My Apprenticeship* helped Webb overcome the depression and paralysis of her war crisis and satisfied her need to create something of her own. Friends applauded the book; the reviewers were unexpectedly enthusiastic. Without violating the documentation of her past that she had in the form of her diary, she managed to create out of her personal history the story of a quest that reached a felicitous end. Synthesis and solution had been achieved: she had found love and work, creed and craft, faith and vocation. Even the debate of the two Egos seemed to have been resolved in the discovery of a 'rational' faith and in the happy combination of service and science.

The writing of *My Apprenticeship* was Webb's response to the public and personal crisis of the First World War, but it was also an expression of many of the impulses and interests that had been stifled within her—with her own compliance—in the years preceding the war. The pleasure she took in the project of her autobiography was unequalled by anything else she had undertaken; for much of the time during the nine years between the beginning and the publication of the book, writing *My Apprenticeship* was all she really cared to do.

This was her own book, written in her own voice and her own style; this was her creation, her 'Work of art,' her novel. For Webb, this autobiography represented an expression of those parts of herself which she considered to be bound up with the artistic, the creative, the religious, the non-rational and even the sexual: she called it 'this child of my old age.' That this autobiography is a work with literary value cannot be an arbitrary proposition. There is a 'special' learning in her statement of her life. Her intelligent and perceptive record of her life is what constitutes the value of *My Apprenticeship*.

***

Webb's Criticism of Her Class

In her early life in her father's home, Webb had found 'labour' an abstract term, used alongside its mate 'capital' and turning up in technical journals and company reports in such revealing phrases as 'water plentiful and labour docile.' In her own words:

> Right down to the time when I began to train as a social investigator, labour was an abstraction, which seemed to denote an arithmetically calculable mass of human beings, each individual a repetition of the other, very much in the same way that the capital of my father's companies consisted, I imagined, of gold sovereigns identical with all other gold sovereigns in form, weight and colour and also in value.[1]

Her imagination getting to work, she realised that this was not a true conception, that 'labour' must consist of individual persons, but she did not feel that the individual persons she met with in her social work were a true sample. Long before she had thought of writing on the trade union or co-operative movements, in 1883 she decided to meet the men and women who composed them. In this first visit, she did not make any deep political generalisations.

But she discovered the co-operative movement and the enormous part played by the dissenting chapels in the life of the Lancashire working class. She also found, a little to her surprise, that she was completely home with these working men and women, that they talked to her freely and in spite of the fact of her smoking cigarettes, found nothing odd about her except that she was far more like a male than a female. Throughout her life, in fact, there was always a large element of what is commonly called masculinity about Webb's mental processes.

The first venture at Bacup led no further for the moment. Webb returned to social work in London. But by this time, she was already disillusioned about the Charity Organisation Society (COS), of which her autobiography contains a full and mordant criticism.

Though Webb worked for COS intermittently for five years, she felt very soon that the stratum of the indigent, the unlucky and the shiftless, with which that body principally dealt, was only the fringe and not a very interesting fringe of 'labour.' Well-to-do men and women of goodwill, who had gone out to offer personal services and friendship to the dwellers in the slums, found themselves transformed into a body of amateur detectives, in some cases initiating prosecutions of persons they thought to be impostors and arousing more suspicion and hatred than the recognised officers of the law. The pioneers of organised charity had made unwittingly an ominous discovery. By tearing off the wrappings of mediaeval society, disguising the skeleton of capitalist civilisation, they had let loose the tragic truth that, whatever society is divided into a minority of 'haves' and a multitude of 'have nots,' charity is twice cursed; it curses him that gives and him that takes.

> Under such circumstances, to quote the phrase of Louise Michel, 'philanthropy is a lie.' For human relationships, whether between individuals, groups or races, do not thrive in an emotional vacuum, if you tune out fellow-feeling and the common consciousness of a social equity, you tune in insolence, envy and 'the wrath that is to come.'[2]

The theory and practice of the COS, in spite of its vogue among those who counted themselves enlightened, found little acceptance among the Christian churches, hardly more than among the impulsive givers of alms.

Thus the COS found itself baulked in its purpose of organising the multifarious charities of the metropolis; neither the churches nor the hospitals, neither the orphanages nor the agencies for providing the destitute with food, clothing or shelter, would have anything to do with a society which sought to impose methods that appeared the very negation of Christian charity. Instead of serving as a co-ordinating body to all the other charities, in order to prevent their harmful overlapping and wasteful competition, the COS became itself the most exclusive of sects, making a merit of disapproving and denouncing much of the practices of other charitable agencies.

The COS had apparently forgotten the experience of its forerunners. Its leading members added to their sectarian creed as to the necessary restrictions of the impulse of charity, an equally determined resistance to any extension of state or municipal action, whether in the way of the physical care of children at school, housing accommodation or medical attendance. In their opinion, modern capitalism was the best of all possible ways of organising industries and services and if only meddlesome persons refrained from interfering with its operations, the maximum social welfare as well as the maximum national wealth would be secured for the whole community. Barring accidents detrimental to life and health, which happens to both rich and poor, any family could, they assumed, maintain its 'independence' from the cradle to the grave, if only its members were reasonably industrious, thrifty, honest, sober and dutiful.

Thus, any attempt by private or public expenditure to alter 'artificially' the economic environment of the manual-working class, so as to lessen the severity of the 'natural' struggle for existence must, they imagined, inevitably undermine these essential elements of personal character. Thus, in the world of philanthropy as in the world of politics, as Webb knew it in the 1880s, there seemed to be one predominant question: 'Were we or were we not to assume the continuance of the capitalist system as it then existed; and if not, could we, by taking thought, mend or end it?'[3]

For a time, Webb found, or thought she had found, a more satisfying field of activity in succeeding her sister Kate as a rent-collector and manager of blocks of working class flats. Here she could observe the people, not as 'failures' applying for charity, but as functioning members of an East End world. As a rent-collector, she hoped to be regarded as part of the normal machinery of the inhabitants' lives, rather than as a detective or an upper-class lady doing a bit of 'slumming.'

The experience, however, was not satisfactory. Webb came to feel increasingly that the whole experiment, of which Katharine Buildings was a part, though it was not like COS detective work—actively insulting the poor—was doing nothing whatever to solve the basic problem: that of their poverty. She went so far as to term it 'an utter failure.' Except as an enlargement of experience, therefore, she must have considered the months she spent in rent-collecting a waste of time, though even here it is instructive to notice the thoroughness with which she set about her job and the instinct for organisation which she brought to bear on it.

Using the headquarters of the "Friends," the Devonshire Hotel in Bishopgate, as her home, she began to assist Booth by making an inquiry into dock labour in town hamlets. What is important here is the influence which the methods, practical and intellectual, of Charles Booth and his able assistants, had on Webb.

The casual observer might be rather surprised to find that a woman of Webb's mental ability, with her immediate personal knowledge of poverty—which nineteenth-century capitalism had produced, enslaving the minds and bodies of its servants, particularly, its women servants—had not become either a socialist or a feminist early in her career. In 1884, she was still writing to a friend, in rather pompous phrasing, of her objection to 'these gigantic experiments, state-education, state-intervention and other matters, which are now being inaugurated and which flavour of inadequately thought-out theories—the most dangerous of all poisons;'[4] even five years later, she had not decided 'whether profit not on the whole demoralising force.'[5]

The demand for women's suffrage reached her from a different source, from ladies of the middle class who were disposed to transform a protest against specific injustices, into a generalised conviction that women as a sex were universally superior to men, but were oppressed by them (which Webb knew to be untrue) and some of whom further extended their equal-rights demand to the abolition of all 'discriminatory' legislation, including the Factory Acts, a demand which Webb rightly thought was monstrous. In sum, it would seem that she had come up against the 'sillier' sort of feminists and that they made her impatient. All her life, Webb was impatient of silliness, more especially when it was exhibited by persons who, because of their birth and education, might reasonably have been expected to know better. She was not a socialist, partly because she had not yet carried her meditations upon social evils which only would have satisfied her, and partly because she had not yet discovered the type of socialist who could appeal to her; she was like a dissatisfied believer who is yet to discover the possibility of atheism. Such socialism as she had come across appeared to her to be the work of doctrinaires, or of ranters, or both. Doctrinairism—an apriorism—she disliked and distrusted instinctively and by the mid-1880s she had already become strongly critical of its particular manifestation in classical political economy.

This was both because it seemed to her to ignore entirely the human element in the production of wealth and further, because its theorisings dealt with only one of many social institutions engaged in or concerned with wealth production. She wanted any study of social questions, whether it was called political economy or whatever else, to be based on and its conclusions to arise from, a study of all social institutions, including the family, trade unions, local governing bodies, churches, etc, in fact, deductive economics needed to be replaced by inductive sociology. It was unfortunate that the socialists whom she came across were of 'the hot-gospeller pure-milk-of-the-word type,'[6] associated with the early days of the Social Democratic Federation and its insistence on the verbal inspiration of *Das Kapital.* She does not say very much about them, but it is clear that she considered them at least as silly as the ardent feminists, if not sillier. And though, by 1888, she had just heard of the Fabian Society, the only Fabian leader she had met was that very 'un-Fabian Fabian,[7] Annie Besant. Her near-acquaintance with the Fabian Society only began when she was referred to another of its leaders as the kind of man who knew everything about social subjects and had the knowledge at his fingertips.

In order to need this man's knowledge, however, she had first to enter the fields in which that knowledge would be useful and this came about through her own explorations. After her work on sweating (a system of subcontracting in the tailoring trade in 19th century England) in the East End was done, she had to decide what she would do with her next 'holiday' from her father's side. Booth made the obvious suggestion that she follow up what she had begun by doing an intensive study of the questions of women's labour in general and should make herself an authority on the subject; and this suggestion was strongly backed by her friend, the economist Alfred Marshall, whom she consulted. But though she seriously considered the idea, she turned it down in favour of a more ambitious plan—to write a book on the co-operative movement. She wanted, in the field of social study, to work on something positive—some of the living institutions ignored by the classical economists. In the co-operative movement, she thought she had found her subject. She knew it was a living and growing thing, as she had seen this with her own eyes. In early 1889, she began work on the book which subsequently appeared as *The Co-operative Movement* and which, despite Marshall's gloomy prophecies, was to hold the field as the only impartial study of its subject for many years to come. Trade unionism—a far bigger subject than Webb could have anticipated in 1889—was the first occupation of the great Webb partnership; but it was their work in the co-operative movement that was directly responsible for the two coming together. The Webbs regularly denounced capitalists as thieves and they looked forward with confidence to an imminent social revolution.

Richard Potter's capitalist ethic and Laurencina Potter's Spencerian dogmas of individualism and laissez-faire formed the dominant orthodoxies of the household, and at the same time, left their daughter with a sense of disturbing ruthlessness and spiritual emptiness. It was the example of her grandparents and of Martha Jackson, the 'household saint,' that offered a set of alternative principles by which to live. Richard Potter Senior and Lawrence Heyworth, her maternal grandfather, were both Northern industrialists, self-made men, 'non-conformists in religion and Radicals in politics,' both elected to Parliament after the Reform Act of 1832. Potter, called 'Radical Dick,' the son of a Yorkshire tenant farmer, had a cotton warehouse in Manchester and supported Free Trade, the Anti-Corn Law League, the abolition of slavery, Catholic Emancipation and the protesters of Peterloo. Heyworth, from a family of Lancashire domestic weavers and cotton hands, prospered as a Liverpool merchant, trading primarily with South America and shared the Radical political sentiments of Richard Potter Senior. Webb describes these two typical representatives of the political and economic developments of nineteenth-century industrial England at the beginning of *My Apprenticeship* not only to suggest something of her parents' origins, but to contrast her grandparents' spirit, their association with community life, their principled and active dedication to the egalitarian thrust of Radicalism with the rootless and seemingly unprincipled atmosphere of her immediate family. The Potter and Heyworth ancestries and their Northern origins, from which Webb's parents had all but cut themselves off, came to represent for her a way of life that held meaning, religious purpose and a true collective and communal spirit. 'I was reared in Toryism,' she once told an interviewer, 'but as I grew up, the Radicalism of my ancestors revived in me.'

In the years following the crisis of 1885–86, Webb continued to profess a Carlylean faith in work as saviour and a Wordsworthian sense that she was fulfilling the mission chosen for her by a power greater than herself. She also continued her self-styled practice of praying and frequented St Paul's for communion services. 'Faith' and 'work' were the constantly recurring keynotes of her diary entries: 'My life must be summed up in the two words: Work and Pray.'[8]

As she wrote her work on co-operation, she grew

closer to an understanding of the need for collectivism, but she still had no direct contact with organised socialists, either the Social Democratic Federation or the newly-created Fabian Society. She began to feel the need for a framework of socialist theory to bolster the objective results of her investigations and she eagerly read a slim volume of essays published by the Fabians in 1889 that had been given to her by a friend.

The essay that most attracted her attention was that written by Sidney Webb because, as she wrote to J C Gray of the co-operative Union in passing the book on to him, 'he has the historic sense.' The concept of 'the inevitability of gradualness' struck a responsive chord in Webb, as she and Sidney Webb shared the same intellectual fathers: Owing mainly to the efforts of Comte, Darwin and Herbert Spencer, wrote Sidney Webb in his Fabian Essay, we can no longer think of the ideal society as an unchanging state. Being static has become dynamic. The social ideal from here on was a socialism that, unlike the English Marxism of the Social Democratic Federation, looked to the Victorian political and social theorists on whom Webb had been raised. Within a very short time of reading these essays, she declared herself, in the pages of her diary, 'a socialist at last.'

Webb's sense of woman's mission to women and her celebration of herself as a single, working female were short-lived and confined to those years of East End involvement, when she was surrounded by others like herself. Her consciousness of herself as an anomalous woman, with all the consequent disadvantages and conflicts, preceded this period of her life and lingered long after it, but her positive enjoyment of her singularity reached a high point during these years and with it increased her sense of solidarity with other women.

The very phenomenon that gave Webb psychological sustenance during those years of East End work, the entry of women like herself into the professions of social service, was, paradoxically, a phenomenon that ultimately contributed to her rejection of a conscious identification with other women despite her earlier sense of solidarity. Webb gradually grew disenchanted with the project of social service, with the professional slots for women that had been created over the last half of the nineteenth century, with what had come to be thought of as women's work. Her temperament and talents moved her away from social work and towards the social investigation she was finally able to do directly, rather than obliquely, with Booth.

As she came to reject the intellectual and ultimately political, constraints of rent-collecting and the supervision of working-class tenants, she also came to reject the mentality of the women with whom she worked. She ceased to conceive of herself as a 'glorified spinster,' as she simultaneously ceased to believe in the legitimacy of the paternalist and individualist premises of the work in which she was engaged. She found that she wanted to do the kind of work that she did not see other women doing, the kind of work she began to do even as a rent collector and which the women around her seemed to understand or appreciate.

It was clear to Webb, after some ten months of work, that the Katherine Buildings project was an 'utter failure.' The rent collectors had little or no salutary effect on the tenants and the tenants who were employed, 'sober' and 'respectable' had little to do with and therefore little influence upon, the tenants who were not. The existence of the people in the buildings had, to Webb's mind, a demoralising and brutalising effect: rowdy tenants disturbed peaceful ones, peaceful ones moved out, boys and girls were forced to socialise at the toilets because the latrines were the only lighted places in the buildings and drunken, out-of-work tenants continued to drink and to be unemployed. 'The lady collectors,' Webb lamented in her diary, 'are an altogether superficial thing.'

She was student enough of Herbert Spencer's to be curious about the lives of institutions, but she was sceptical enough of his theories to want to leave them in abeyance until the process of investigation was completed. Webb felt sure of her own 'audacity of mind,' but she despaired her lack of method and her ignorance of history. She planned to write an analysis and her ignorance of history. She planned to write an analysis of 'social diagnosis,' and towards this end, began a campaign of historical study.

Webb entered into professional life in the company of middle-class Victorian women whose aim was service, but she had authentic ancestors among the women writers of the 1830s, 1840s and 1850s whose aim was 'continuous enquiry: investigation and instruction.' These women, most of whom wrote about Manchester and the smaller industrial towns of Lancashire, attempted to describe the way working-class people lived and, even more importantly, the way they worked. The nature of occupations, the conditions of labour and the processes of manufacturing attracted their interest and formed the subjects for their novels, tales and articles. Women such as Jane Narcot, Charlotte Tonna and Harriet Martineau combined an interest in the dynamics of industrial life with a desire to educate the middle-class public by translating the abstractions of political economy into the concrete details of daily life and work.

They added a didactic temper to the study of Parliamentary Blue Books and personal observation and they formed a bridge between the eighteenth-century women writers of moral tales—Hanna More, Mrs Barbauld and Maria Edgeworth—and the novelists of industrial life who dominated the middle decades of the nineteenth century—Gaskell, Disraeli, Dickens and Kingsley.[9]

A NUMBER of women writers—Caroline Norton, Frances Trolloppe, Elizabeth Barett Browning and Elizabeth Gaskell—were moved to write on the subject of industrial life out of a desire to expose the devastating conditions to which working people were subjected and to promote a spirit of middle-class sympathy. These women were, by talent or vocation, novelists and poets who devoted one or two or their numerous literary efforts to the plight of the industrial labourer.

Webb also believed in the salutary purposes of fiction and she was periodically tempted, throughout the decade on the 1880s, to write a novel. Her first commitment was always to the revelation of man's social nature and to the investigation of his social relationships, but she believed that throughout the nineteenth century the writers of fiction had been among the only true social investigators. 'For any detailed description of the complexity of human nature,' she writes in *My Apprenticeship*, 'of the variety and mixture in human motive, of the insurgence of instinct in the garb of reason, of the multifarious play of the social environment on the individual and of the individual ego on the social environment, I had to turn to novelists and poets, to Fielding and Flaubert, to Thackeray and Goethe.' She began to record 'realistic scenes of country and town life' in her diary in the early years of the 1880s, to write 'analytic portraits of relations and friends and to record social encounters in dramatic form.'

For Webb, the spring of 1886 was a time of methodological and personal experimentation, a period of professional and political transformation. The methodological innovations of Booth's study and the work Webb contributed to it, expressed an ideological deviation from certain dominant middle-class attitudes towards poverty and the poor. The work of Octavia Hill, the settlement house of Samuel Barnett and the East End sojourn of Edward Denison all implied that the correct relationship between rich and poor ought to be one of close personal contact, in the interest of replacing the relationship of the 'cash nexus' with one of human sympathy and of imbuing the 'lower' classes with middle-class knowledge, habits and values. Booth's work suggested a re-definition of the ideal relationship between classes, a decision to find out about the way working-class people lived, for the purpose of furthering reform without having any direct, personal impact on the individual poor. Scientific knowledge of a class, rather than personal influence brought to bear on individuals, would bring about desired social change.

In Booth's scheme, it was, in fact, the middle-class observer who would be transformed through contact with the working class and would then go on to promote reform. Statistical analysis and personal observation were the primary elements of Booth's and Webb's methods for obtaining such scientific knowledge, but the problem for them was to carry out observation without having any effect on those observed. This was achieved by Webb through disguise and by Booth through the anonymous occupancy of working-class lodgings during the time of his investigation.[10]

For Webb, it was the breaking down of acquired prejudice and clan biases through the use of disguise and the temporary redefinition of class identity that made ideological change possible. As a result of investigation and an altered class perspective, she arrived at political solutions that were heretical within the context of her Individualist training. Private identification with working-class individuals, brought about because of personal and professional needs, led to the public espousal of methods for protecting that class. She was also engaged in sampling various political ideologies, all quite different from her own, as a way of exploring solutions to the real problems—unemployment and casual labour—that she was confronting at the docks. She believed that the social investigator had an obligation to arrive at political or ideological conclusions, that he or she should work synthetically as well as empirically. Booth and Webb did, after all, embark upon investigation as a method to promote reform; however, though social change may have been an implicit goal of his work, Booth did not enter into his investigations with reform as an explicit aim. Booth believed that, in many cases, he could complete his role as investigator by placing 'facts' before the men of politics and power, but Webb felt a responsibility and a desire, to reach a destination and to present it to her audience. She tried to be descriptive, analytic and prescriptive and Booth did not always agree with what she perceived to be the scope of her role as investigator.

Webb was not wholly satisfied with her study of dock labour. She estimated that it was an 'inferior piece of work,' not exhaustive enough and too quickly written. When she began her research on the 'sweating system,' she decided to go beyond the method of her first essay by performing an 'experiment in the craft of social investigation. She would train as a trouser-hand, live among the 'actual workers' and thereby prepare herself to 'present a picture' of work and life in an East End tailor's shop. Webb believed that she had discovered more about dock-workers as an inconspicuous rent collector in Katherine Buildings than she had as a recognisable investigator touring the docks or the labourers' houses.

Although both observation with the use of disguise and scientific social investigation without it shared the virtue of not interfering with the lives of those observed or investigated, for Webb they differed in one essential characteristic: disguise allowed for—and expressed—a sympathetic identification with the people observed, while social investigation demanded the exercise of a critical spirit.

One of the most revealing comments that Webb made on the use of disguise was a brief one in a letter to Richard Potter. She remarked that 'the only way to understand these people is, for the time, to adopt their faith and look at things in their light.' 'Then,' she continued, 'one gets a clear picture, undisturbed by any critically antagonistic spirit, of their life, both material and mental.'[11] Webb suggests here that only through disguise can she become totally empathetic with the people she wants to investigate. Clothed and represented as herself, she would automatically assume a 'critically antagonistic' posture. For Webb, to be an investigator, to be analytic and scientific, was to be in opposition; objectivity meant, to her, the ability to be 'equally censorious and ideological' about everyone.

Webb's anti-Individualist suggestions were both more practical than Booth's and more directly aimed at the problem that had been uncovered at the base of poverty: the conditions of labour. Modern critics have pointed out that among Booth's failures was his inability to apply the idea of State intervention to the area of employment and to make recommendations that could be taken seriously by politicians and the press. Webb's proposals, on the other hand, for a possible amalgamation of the London docks under a Public Trust, for increased organisation of workers and for the extension of factory legislation to cover unregulated workplaces and unprotected workers were specifically directed at problems of employment and were eminently practicable. Booth wanted to apply Socialistic measures only to those who could not, apparently, fend for themselves and whose inability to do so supposedly contributed to the demoralisation of other workers around them. Webb wanted to apply such measures to the conditions that affected all workers. Booth seemed more anxious to attack the effects of poverty and Webb its causes. Because of the peculiar quality of her intelligence and the peculiar nature of her relation to her times, she gave special attention to the main features of the upper class, describing the main social currents, in her original way that was not possible for others. In terms of consciousness about matters of human experience and the problems implicit in it, she resembles John Stuart Mill, who could be said to be her predecessor as a disciplined thinker, as a trained logician and as an analyst. In the early chapters of *My Apprenticeship*, she presents a profound sense of the heterogeneous social environments—and of the class that gives orders, is the idol of personal power in the London Society, concomitant with the decay of Christianity and is characterised by intellectual chaos.

***

Portrait of an Ethos

If *My Apprenticeship* belongs to a classic tradition of Victorian autobiography as well as to the tradition of nineteenth-century women's writing, it does so largely because of the life Webb was able to live in the last decades of the Victorian age. The shape of Webb's search for what she called 'creed' and 'craft' was determined by the convergence of certain historical phenomena of those decades—by changes in the position of women, by the 'discovery' of poverty in the East End of London, by new kinds of social investigation and by the 'socialist revival' at the end of the century. By looking at the two 'apprenticeships,' we begin to understand some of the ways in which history gives form to individual life and in turn, influences the use of literary genre. If, as Carlyle wrote, 'History is the essence of innumerable Biographies,' then the history of the Victorian age may be regarded as the essence of innumerable autobiographies.

The autobiographies of a number of Victorians

belong to a secular tradition. Webb's *My Apprenticeship* belongs to this Victorian autobiographical tradition.

What is Webb's sense of the Victorian age? Her analysis, exposition and evaluation of this age characterise the mind that is concerned with the 'ethos' of the age. In the introduction to *My Apprenticeship*, Webb writes that beneath the surface of daily existence, her life had been determined by an opposition, a 'continuous controversy between an Ego that affirms and an Ego that denies.' With this phrase she signals an entry into the familiar world of Victorian dichotomies. Her brief discussion of the two questions generated by the continuous controversy between the two Egos defines the obsessions of mind and spirit that dominate her autobiography and dominated her life. The first question raises the possibility of a science of society. The second and more intensely personal of the two, involves the need for religion to determine the ideals on which society will be based:

> ...assuming that there will be, or will be, such a science of society, is man's capacity for scientific discovery the only faculty required for the reorganisation of society according to an ideal? or do we need religion as well as science, emotional faith, as well as intellectual curiosity?[1]

The affirming Ego believes in both the efficacy of social science and the additional need for a religious ideal to give ethical direction to science. The denying Ego is the doubter, the sceptic, who questions the value of both religious faith and social science.

The account of young Webb's early training (and the consequent spiritual crisis) has itself a direct bearing to the study of the Victorian age. Besides, the account of her intellectual life, which forms the main part of the book, is a very penetrating analysis of Victorian history. This was made possible by the fact that that she belonged to the 'intellectual milieu,' very central to the Victorian age—which included Mill and George Eliot.

Dickens put the railway at the centre of *Dombey and Son*, a novel that exposes the confusion of business morality with human morality, the way in which family life is corroded by the ethic of the 'cash nexus.' There is a symbolic appropriateness to Richard Potter's involvement with the railway, that emblem of the equivocal nature of Victorian Progress. The constant change and movement of the Potter household and the ambition, unencumbered by ethics, of Richard Potter, are understood in Dickens' vision of the effects of industrial capitalism on family life.[2]

At the beginning of the nineteenth century, a new and penetrating voice began to make itself heard, the voice of science. Scientific theories and concepts were discussed by people who had hitherto given them but little attention. It would have been difficult for the people to remain indifferent to science, which was so rapidly transforming their lives. Webb was a social scientist. The Victorian age was, within certain limits, conspicuously religious. In the 1870s, Webb experienced an adolescent depression and consequently had a brief engagement with hardline Christianity. Although this conversion was promptly followed by a loss of faith, she continued to feel the need to find 'a creed by which I could live.' This crisis ended in a renewed commitment to vocation. It marked the beginning of her apprenticeship as a social investigator. In 1874, at the age of 16, Webb remarked in her notes on Faust that his resolve to commit suicide is broken 'by the feeling which the church bells and the songs of the choir on Easter morning awaken in him.' In the following months, her own life would seem to mimic in adolescent fashion the pattern she perceived in Faust: a painful period of unhappiness and illness would end in a phase of extreme Christian devotion. A few months after she had begun to translate Faust, she resolved to 'make a faith' for herself. Following, in her own manner, the pattern of Faust, she received the Holy Sacrament for the first time at Easter, 1875. She reached a height of religious devotion and solemnity that transformed even the language and tone of her diary:

> Eastern Eve: The day before I received for the first time the Holy Sacrament. The last month or two has been a very solemn epoch in my life and may God grant that I may never cease remembering the vows which I have made before God and man, that I intend to become a true Christian, that is, a true disciple and follower of Jesus Christ, making Him my sole aim in life. And now I am going to receive the

> great sacrament, which He Himself, instituted as a perpetual means of remembering His visit on earth.[3]

By the winter of 1875–76, Webb had begun to struggle with growing doubts about certain aspects of Christian dogma and her orthodoxy had begun to wane. She perceived in Spencer's philosophy not only a divinity to worship, but a true marriage of religion and science. She found that she had an inclination to doubt materialism more than spiritualism.

The controversy between the two Egos was moving toward a temporary resolution: Webb was still looking for a Church. The death of her mother in 1882 found her ready for a renewal of religious faith and pushed her towards the refuge of prayer and work. In the years following the crisis of 1885–86, Webb continued to profess a Carlylean faith in work as a saviour and a Wordsworthian sense that she was fulfilling the mission chosen for her by a power greater than herself. 'Faith' and 'work' were the constantly recuring keynotes of her diary entries. The Victorian notion of vocation-of-faith, coupled with work for the good of humanity, evolved in her consciousness as she emerged from her 'silent agony' of 1885–86.

During these 'years of apprenticeship,' when faith and work set the tone of her daily life, Webb discovered her vocation and, in so doing, began the gradual conversion to socialism; that is the central theme of *My Apprenticeship*. This conversion, from individualism to collectivism, had its roots in her rejection of the ethos of her home. The faith toward which she gravitated was generated out of the work she did in the 1880s and out of the political temper of the decade. Her crisis of the 1880s ended in a commitment to the work of social investigation and a translation of the remnants of Christian faith into the 'faith' of socialism.

Webb adopted her vocation in the atmosphere of what she calls the 'mid-Victorian Time-Spirit,' a spirit that combined belief in the powers of science with the 'impulse of self-subordinating service... transferred, consciously and overtly, from God to man':

> It is hard to understand the naive belief of the most original and vigorous minds of the 'seventies' and 'eighties' that it was by science and by science alone, that all human misery would be ultimately swept away.[4]

Science could demonstrate how the purpose of life might be fulfilled and the purpose itself would be determined by this transfer of the impulse of service from God to Society. If science was to be the method and service the purpose, Webb drew the inference that the most hopeful form of social service was the craft of a social investigator. August Comte represented to Webb a culmination of the mid-Victorian Time-Spirit. The unification of a glorification of science with a 'religion of humanity' suited Victorian intellectual needs and made the science of society appear a logical and morally justified vocation. The mid-Victorian Time-Spirit and the 'consciousness of sin' that pervaded certain sections of Webb's own class made 'slumming' and charity work likely activities for a young woman looking for some way of translating what she had learned at her own desk into useful action. During the London Season of 1883, Webb became a philanthropic 'case-worker,' visiting the homes of the poor, in order to determine which families were 'deserving' and which 'undeserving' of charitable assistance from private organisations.

She was attracted to this work with the COS because of its ostensibly 'scientific approach' to the problem of poverty. As Mill struggled between Bentham and Coleridge, Webb struggled between a spirit of affirmation and a spirit of denial of faith and scepticism, the two being the precepts of the Victorian period.

As Carlyle eschewed the celebrations of selfhood and embraced the celebrations of work and duty, so did Webb. And like Gosse, White and Mill, she rebelled against an inherited set of principles associated with a parental lack of feeling, of tenderness, of true spirituality, growing up in an age that clearly separated the spheres of men and women, she found it all but impossible to reconcile her longings for public achievement with her desire for the private happiness of marriage and domesticity. Like Fuller and like so many other accomplished Victorian women, she could not understand two seemingly irreconcilable impulses. *My Apprenticeship* shares this theme of division with memoirs of other nineteenth-century women and with some of the major works of fiction by Victorian women novelists, and in its own way, it represents an amalgam of these two genres of women's writing. She neither intended to 'fictionalise' her life nor make her private life the content of her work. And for most nineteenth-century women of ambition and achievement, the resolution of struggle and the satisfactory discovery of sexual and spiritual identity remained painfully elusive and, therefore, virtually impossible to describe.

It was as necessary to the Victorian woman's survival to keep an inner life of conflict masked as it was to keep illegitimate aspirations hidden. How to have a 'thorough experience of life' without violating the rules that circumscribed a Victorian woman's sphere of activity was a question often solved temporarily by the embracing of religious devotion. Once the right to activity was won, it became nearly impossible to reconcile that activity with the more traditional destinies of women. Webb experienced her failure to be an ordinary woman as a conflict between 'masculine' and 'feminine' selves. In her autobiography, this conflict of sexual identity intersects with a specific spirited conflict—between the believing 'Ego' and the sceptical 'Ego'—that characterises the autobiographies of numerous male Victorians. The womanly aspect of her nature, the, faculty of faith and 'emotive thought'—a term she owed to George Eliot—had to be incorporated into whatever philosophy she adopted and whatever action she undertook. Webb sought to resolve the convergent crises of faith and sexual identity in a mode of existence that would combine 'manly' scepticism and 'womanly' belief, public striving and private contentment.

The problems of the anomalous female that regularly appear in the memoirs of nineteenth-century women are also found in Webb's autobiography: the sense of inner division, the elusiveness of integration of self, the struggle against fantasy, the self-admonishment for vanity and egoism, the difficulties of study and work, the question of marriage and its tyrannies. In *My Apprenticeship*, however, these separate problems are raised to the level of structure-giving themes, as they are in the autobiographical novels of Bronte and George Eliot.

Webb took excerpts from her diary, the private note-books in which she wrote for seventy years and the equivalent of many of the unstructured memoirs written by nineteenth-century women and wove them into a thematically coherent whole, interpreting them by creating from them a pattern and teleological form. The conflicts expressed in these diary passages are resolved in *My Apprenticeship*, as they are not in the memoirs of Martineau, Nightingale, Besant, Addams and Sand. As male Victorians resolved spiritual and intellectual crises in their autobiographies, as Bronte and Eliot resolved—however problematically—the conflicts of their heroines, so did Webb depict the integration of her divided self, the resolutions of her sexual and spiritual struggles, in the denouement of *My Apprenticeship*. As conversion to Fabianism, a political philosophy that ostensibly accommodated both science and faith, transcends the struggle, between the two 'Egos,' so marriage to Sidney Webb, a husband who was also a partner in work and faith, transcends the conflict between the 'masculine' and 'feminine' selves.

Long before she developed the political and social critique of her society which redeemed her from the 'occupational disease' of the London 'Season,' Webb found the antidote to variety in religion. The moral flaws she detected in those 'present religious systems' prevented her from adopting any one of them as her own, but did not stop her from expressing the impulses of her 'emotive thought' in prayer.

She acted as her father's companion in business and as her youngest sister's guardian. She also had to spend her time entertaining and being entertained by the social circle to which she belonged. The only legitimate counter-claim on her time that was recognised by the society in which Webb lived was the making of a 'good marriage,' the 'masterpiece' to which this apprenticeship of social exercise was to lead. How could she reconcile the rival pulls on time and energy, on the one hand, of family affection, backed up by the Victorian code of domesticity; and, on the other, of a domineering curiosity into the nature of things, reinforced by an awakening desire for creative thought and literary expression?[5] Her frantic attempt to combine three or four lives in one gave her a feeling of schizophrenia, altered her books and caused that sense of division as common among the heroines of fiction and the writers of memoirs. Webb's 'real life' was all internal, her external life all empty movement. The life of thought was her 'real life,' the power that dominated her existence. If plagues of vanity and daydreaming, the embracing of religious commitment, the plight of the unmarried daughter, rejections of marriage proposals and periods of emotional and physical collapse are familiar to the reader of nineteenth-century women's memoirs, the neat resolutions of life and literary structure of Webb's *My Apprenticeship* are not.

The split between the spiritual and physical needs of women, as it is so clearly depicted by Charlotte Bronte in *Jane Eyre* and George Eliot in *The Mill on the Floss*, is transcended in Bronte's *Villette* in its uniting of love and work, relationship and authenticity of self. In marrying Sidney Webb, Beatrice Potter was striving for that kind of transcendence. Fabianism allowed for a synthesis of her need for faith, which she thought a 'feminine' need and her scientific scepticism, which she thought a 'masculine' faculty. So did her marriage to Sidney Webb allow for a synthesis of her 'feminine' desire for private fulfillment and her 'masculine' desire to analyse, write and work.

As explained in Chapter 1, *My Apprenticeship* belongs to the tradition of Victorian autobiography because of the nature of its content. Webb was able to imagine her life according to a specific model of human growth and to write a certain genre of autobiography because the facts of history allowed her to find vocation and achieve reconciliation. Political events, economic crises and intellectual movements form the subjects of *My Apprenticeship* and are the reasons for its very existence.

Whether we read the fun and sentiment of Dickens, the social miniatures of Thackeray, or the psychological studies of George Eliot, we find in almost every case a definite purpose to sweep away error and to reveal the underlying truth of human life. So the novel sought to do for society in this age precisely what Lyell and Darwin sought to do for science. This is what has been sought in *My Apprenticeship*. Perhaps for this reason the Victorian Age is emphatically an age of realism rather than of romance—not the realism of Zola and Ibsen, but a deeper realism which strives to tell the whole truth, showing moral and physical diseases as they are, but holding up wealth and hope as the normal conditions of humanity. Webb's own private life proves to be an example of this Victorian code.

Webb had abandoned abstract theory for a synthesis of empiricism and historical method, where one is able to trace the typical Victorian touch. Her rejection of more traditional women's work and her ultimate dedication to the empirical Sociology of Booth helped to determine her peculiarly ambivalent relationship to late-nineteenth-century feminism. By the middle decades of the nineteenth century, large numbers of middle-and upper-class women had become active in the areas of social reform that involved poverty, health and education. Webb was no exception to it. When Hippolyte Taine visited England in 1861–62, he was struck by the serious and sober preoccupations of the females of that nation and was impressed by the articles on social issues he found in *The English Women's Review* and in the publication of the National Association for the Promotion of Social Service.

Philanthropic work provided socially acceptable and useful activity for middle-class women and posed no threat to the conventional separation between male and female spheres of labour; it involved women in public work, but only as an extension of private duties. By the last decades of the century, however, it had become clear that the ethic of female charity had provided women with a legitimate entry into various professional fields.

The 'discovery' of poverty in the last decades of the century seems to have provided new and more numerous 'loopholes' as a result of the proliferation of organisations and institutions created in response to this 'discovery.' COS and the Salvation Army were organisations to which women gravitated and which were particularly receptive to their participation. In 1882, following the example of her sister Kate, Webb started working for Society. She herself ascribed the zeal to a 'class-consciousness of sin' among property-owners, arising from the violent contrasts in standards of living between rich and poor, which produced the thunder of Carlyle and the outspoken pictures of Dickens; but it is probable that the causes lie further back. She was appalled by the high amateurism of the English elite. She complained that while the standard of natural ability in political life was remarkably high, the standard of acquirements was ludicrously low.

The distinction between politics and administration, though she no doubt acknowledged it in theory, was not vivid to her. Her constant cry seemed to be, 'Find the facts, decide what actions will best ameliorate them, then carry out the policy.' But this tendency to oversimplify the political process did not by any means make her inflexible. Clearly, she thought hard about her status as a woman in a world of men and a woman who had not in the least been de-feminised by hard political work.

Webb agreed to replace her married sister Kate, not because of an urgent sympathy with the poor, but because poverty seemed to her a live and controversial issue and because her reading of social thought—of Spencer, Comte and Mill—convinced her that the issue could be solved not in the realm of theory but in the observation of human beings in their daily life or working lives. She found that Comte's appeal for her and for other English disciples lay in his 'union of the "religion of humanity" with a glorification of science.' That union, she maintained in *My Apprenticeship*, epitomised the 'mid-Victorian Time Spirit.' She first came to Comte through the writings of those considered to be his most important English disciples and admirers—George Henry Lewes, John Stuart Mill and George Eliot.

Webb's positing of an antithetical relationship between sexuality and socialism was not, of course, peculiar to her, but it was wholly consistent with the dichotomies, confusions and conflations that characterised the Victorian period. Why did she wish to relegate responsibility for individual morality to an absolute authority, and why did she confuse morality with asceticism? We can answer that all of this moralism is but a reflection of what we have come to call 'Victorianism,' but we can also recognise in Webb the individual dynamics of personality and circumstance that made her peculiarly susceptible to this aspect of 'Victorianism.'

In *My Apprenticeship*, as distinguished from the diary, conflict and contradiction were not only exposed but transcended. Webb chose an autobiographical form that gave intellectual and spiritual debate a central role, a place of prominence. The careful reader of *My Apprenticeship* must reject the 'grim inhuman (Webb) legend... of infallibility... (and)... omniscience' and put in its place a Webb vexed by the problems of what to believe and what to be, of faith and identity. But if she chose this Victorian genre because it allowed her to expose conflict and inner debate, she also chose it for its insistence upon reconciliation and resolution. The reader of this autobiography soon realises how little of the story of Webb consists of the personal details which bulk so large in the lives of most eminent women. Her life-history is the social history of two generations.

Herbert Spencer's failure to attain the higher levels of conduct and feeling had sealed Webb's conviction in the bankruptcy of science when it attempted to realize the cause or the aim of human existence. 'The fitfulness, suspicion, pretty irritations and antagonisms which have disfigured the later years have,... increased my distaste for all varieties of utilitarian ethics, all attempts to apply the scientific method, to the *Purpose* as distinguished from the *Processes* of existence[6],' she wrote emphatically. Herbert Spencer's failure to attain the higher levels of conduct and feeling had sealed Webb's conviction in the bankruptcy of science when it attempted to realise the cause or the aim of human existence. According to Webb, London society appeared to be centres of social circles representing or epitomising certain dominant forces within the British governing class.

There was the court, representing national tradition and custom. There was a mysterious group of millionaire financiers representing money. There was the cabinet and ex-cabinet, representing political power. All persons who habitually entertained and who were entertained by the members of any one of these key groups could claim to belong to London society. These four inner circles crossed and recrossed each other owing to an element of common membership, this in the 'seventies and eighties' happening to consist of striking personalities.

British aristocracy was the most talented, the most energetic and the most vulgar in the world. The bulk of the shifting mass of wealthy persons who were conscious of belonging to London society, who practised its rites and followed its fashions, were, in the last quarter of the nineteenth century, professional profit-makers. The first and foremost characteristic of the London season and country-house life, a characteristic which distinguished it from the recreation and social intercourse of the rest of the community, was the fact that some of the men and practically all the women made the pursuit of pleasure their main occupation in life. Riding, dancing, flirting and dressing up, the pleasurable but somewhat feverish anticipation of endless distraction, a dissipation of mental and physical energy, filled up the hours of the day and lasted far into the night. Meanwhile, as one form of entertainment was piled on another, the pace became fast and furious; a mania for reckless talking, for the experimental display of one's own personality, ousted all else from consciousness.

Incidentally, Webb discovered that personal vanity was an 'occupational disease' of London society. A distressing mental nausea, taking the form of cynicism about one's own and other people's character, had destroyed all faith in and capacity for steady work. There was no steadfastness about manners, morals or intellectual gifts. Personal wealth was, however, only one of the many different types of power accepted as a passport to good society. The same worship of power was shown in the suppression of one type of person by another. It was this continuous uncertainty as to social status that led to 'all the ugly methods of entertaining practised by the crowd who wanted to get into society.' Thus, the dominant impulse was neither the greed of riches nor the enjoyment of luxurious living, though both these motives were present, but the desire for power. Christian tradition in the 1870s and 1880s had grown thin and brittle, more easily broken than repaired. People lived indeed in a perpetual state of ferment, receiving and questioning all contemporary hypotheses as to the duty and destiny of man in this world and the next. Into this all-questioning state of mind were thrust the two most characteristic of current assumptions: first, that physical science could solve all problems; and secondly, that everyone, aided by a few elementary textbooks, could be his own philosopher and scientist. Such was the penetrating analysis of Victorian history presented by Webb in *My Apprenticeship*.

***

Webb's Interest in the Working Class

How did Webb come to have interest in the working class? What is so peculiar is that she was interested in this movement, being a woman of the upper class and her work therefore has an attraction to the reader. Amidst the tyranny of the class society over the individuals. Webb looked forward to a socialist system favourable to the working class. Her dilemma in choosing a craft, being torn between conflicting aims, makes her finally come to an important decision of being a social investigator. Webb spent her childhood in a quite special way among domestic servants, to whom as a class she had an undying gratitude.

Webb's sister Kate, after an apprenticeship under Octavia Hill, had become a rent-collector in Whitechapel. It was while staying with Kate in London that Webb first became aware of the meaning of the poverty of the poor. If she had any vain regrets for absent opportunities, it was exactly this: that she grew up to maturity as a sociological investigator without a spell of observation and experiment in the modern science of psychology. She read Spencer for the first time, not as a social scientist, not as a scientific guide to the evolution and organisation of society, but as the proponent of a substitute religion. She perceived in Spencer's philosophy not only a divinity to worship, but a true marriage of religion and science. Spencer's theories, because of what she sought in them, could not long sustain her, and in the final years of the 1870s and the first years of the 1880s, she was bothered by an awareness that she lacked the kind of real faith that would support her in times of unhappiness. Spencer's 'unknowable' provided insufficient comfort. Ultimately she came to reject his laissez-faire bias as the most glaring fault of his social analysis, but among her first reasons for questioning Spencer's wisdom was what she later called his 'materialism.' She found that she had 'an inclination to doubt materialism more than... spiritualism.'

Webb does record in the autobiography, however, in words recalling both Mill's and Carlyle's rejection of the goal of happiness, a newfound determination to begin to live for others and take 'what happiness comes to us by the way.' The path of personal happiness and gratification having been blocked, she decided to make service and work her goals. But this decision too was thwarted. Her father suffered a stroke and Webb was tied to home as his nurse and constant companion. The experience of work ceased to be available to her. She found herself with neither the fulfillment of personal relationship nor the satisfaction of useful activity; her despair and dejection reached Coleridgean proportions. She read St. Augustine, continued the self-training of a student society by reading history and philosophy and fortified herself to renounce not only the worldly life of London society but the possibility of private happiness as wife and mother.

It was in the disguise of Miss Jones, a farmer's daughter, that Webb went in November 1883 to stay in the house of John Ashworth in a back street of Bacup in Lancashire and there to meet, long before she had thought of writing on the trade union or cooperative movements, the men and women who composed them. The cotton operatives of Bacup was the stepping stone for her entry in trade union activities. We can sense her development in the record of their moral refinement and the reality of their religion.

> When I was at Bacup (I mediate after my first visit) I felt as if I were living through a page of puritan history: felt that I saw the actual thing, human beings governed by one idea; devotion to Christ, with no struggle or thought about the world; in every action of their daily living unto God. And I realised the strength of the motive which enlightened persons believe is passing away. I realised the permeating influence and wondered what would fill the void it would leave, what inspiring motive would take its place?[1]

The Bacup adventure gave a decisive turn to Webb's self-development.

> Everyday actual observation of men and things takes the place of accumulation of facts from books and boudoir trains of thought. Undoubtedly the Bacup trip is the right direction. To profit by that kind of observation I must gain more knowledge of legal and commercial matters, understand the theory of government before I can appreciate deficiencies in practice. The time is come now for a defined object towards which all my energies must be bent.[2]

The die was cast; the craft was chosen. Through the pressure of circumstances and the inspiration of the time-spirit, Webb had decided to become an investigator of social institutions. In November 1885, she produced a proposal for the association of all the agencies which provided housing for the poor, covering about 150,000 persons, for the pooling of all the information which they could collect about the objects of their charity. This, however, she could never complete, as she was forced to look after her father who became ill suddenly. When her sisters decided to relieve her, it was not to rent-collecting that she returned, but to help Charles Booth in his great inquiry into the life and labour of the people of London.

In the years of her apprenticeship (1883–1887), the COS appeared to Webb as an honest though short-sighted attempt to apply the scientific method of observation and experiment, reasoning and verification, to the task of delivering the poor from their miseries by the personal service and pecuniary assistance tendered by their leisured and wealthy fellow citizens. The leading spirits of the COS, when she first came across it in 1883, had been its principal founders Octavia Hill, Samuel Barnett, W H Fremantle and C S Loch. Such was Webb's intellectual environment—the then closely interrelated worlds of politics and metropolitan philanthropy.

Charles Booth came under the influence of Auguste Comte. He had the scientific impulse, in his case directed towards the structure and working of society. Charles Booth was singularly appreciative of any suggestions, however irrelevant or far-fetched these might seem, from fellow-workers and subordinates. Webb was of the opinion that Charles Booth was the union of faith in the scientific method with the transference of the emotion of self-sacrificing service from God to man. Booth interested Webb as a man who had his nature completely under control.

In 1877, Webb began to assist Charles Booth in his mammoth study of the life and labour of the people of London, a project which combined, for the first time, qualitative and quantitative methods of sociological study. Webb learned her vocation as an observer of dock-workers, the sweating-system and the Jewish community of East London and, as she mastered her vocation, she moved farther and farther away from the politics and economics of individualism. Booth and his assistants, having originally undertaken to prove that poverty was not as rampant in London as socialists and 'sensationalists' had been arguing, succeeded instead in exposing a degree of poverty that no one else had yet imagined. The question that had to be asked then was: 'How had this morass of destitution and chronic poverty arisen during a period of unprecedented national prosperity?' The answer was to be found in the conditions of employment of the people and not in the devil drink, the influx of 'aliens' (Jews) into the East End, the insidious effects of indiscriminate charity or in the innate degeneracy of the lower classes. Webb herself concluded that 'uncontrolled competition' and 'individualism run wild' had to be checked by legislation, by the organisation of labourers and by certain limited kinds of municipal socialism.

Webb sought an explanation for the differences between the conditions of the 'sweated workers of East London and the Lancashire textiles operatives' and found it in the collective regulation of the conditions of employment, by either legislative enactments or collective bargaining (the latter term being her own brainchild). She had recognised the importance of co-operation in the lives of the Bacup workers, and she now realised that it exemplified the will to self-government that she had found lacking among the workers of the East End. Was there any 'practical alternative,' she wondered, 'to the dictatorship of the capitalist in industry?' Did co-operative societies fulfil the ideal of self-employment and successfully eliminate the role of the capitalist entrepreneur? She discovered that the outstanding achievement of the co-operative movement was the organisation of industry 'from the consumption end,' under the collective control of workers as producer consumers.

Webb was beginning to discover how working-class people perceived social reality as well as how they worked. She was also engaged in sampling various political ideologies, all quite different from her own, as way of exploring solutions to the real problems of unemployment and casual labour that she was confronting at the docks. She found her 'East End experiences' 'easy and pleasant, but...all froth.' She believed that the social investigator had an obligation to arrive at political or ideological conclusions, that or she should work synthetically as well as empirically. Booth and Webb did, after all, embark upon investigation as a method to promote reform. Booth believed that, in many cases, he could complete his role as investigator by placing 'facts' before the men of politics and power, but Webb felt responsibility and a desire to reach the 'destination' and to present it to her audience.

Webb tried to be descriptive, analytic and prescriptive, and Booth did not always agree with what she perceived to be the scope of her role as investigator. Webb's essays on the docks, which appeared in 1887 as *The Dock Life of East London*, marks a change from the strict individualist perspective of her 'Lady's view of the unemployed' and brings her at least a step closer to a collectivist solution to social problems. Webb was one of a number of observers at that time who were writing and talking about the crisis of the docks, the decline of the industry, the wild competition among employers and the oversupply of labour. Webb was a new kind of critic, one who employed facts to show things as they are and described the dock labourers as neither 'ne'er-do-wells' nor 'downfallen angels,' but in terms of 'all sorts and conditions' of men. For Webb, the history and development of any social problem or institution was always essential. Her essay on dock labour is a hybrid of perspectives, an expression of her transitional and fluctuating point of view. The rigid hierarchy of labour, according to Webb, created antagonism between the different 'classes' of employees and bred an isolation of workers that damages the social life of the East End community. The social dislocation that she observed in working-class London contributed, she believed, to the demoralisation of this class, as did the irregularity of employment. Here, Webb made a significant contribution to the understanding of the 'culture' of poverty.

Webb was not wholly satisfied with her study of dock labour. She estimated that it was an 'inferior piece of work,' not exhaustive enough and too quickly written. When she began her research on the 'sweating system,' she decided to go beyond the method of her first essay by performing an experiment in the craft of social investigation. She would train as a trouser-hand (one who makes trousers), live among the 'actual workers' and thereby prepare herself to 'present a picture' of work and life in an East End tailor's shop.[3] Webb believed that she had discovered more about dock-workers as an inconspicuous rent-collector in Katherine buildings than she had as a recognisable investigator touring the docks or the labourers' houses. Besides she had already used the technique of disguise when she visited Bacup, a small manufacturing town in Lancashire in 1883. That experiment had proved a personal and professional success. The trip to Bacup and her disguise as the social equal of its inhabitants had a personal as well as a professional purpose.

The journey to Bacup was also a gesture at reclaiming an intimate tie with her mother. She went a second time before she began her work with Booth in 1886, when she revealed her identity, and again in 1889, before she started to write her study of co-operation. Bacup became for her a kind of touchstone against which to measure all other working-class communities.

The split between love and work, between private and public existence, that Webb found so problematic in her own life did not seem to her to trouble the lives of factory operatives. Meanwhile the second part of Charles Booth's plan of campaign, relating to the occupations of the people—'how they work' as distinguished from 'how they live'—was proceeding. There was at first a trial trip in which Webb co-operated. This concerned the conditions of employment and the industries peculiarly associated with the East End of London, such as labour in the London docks and wharves, various branches of what was called the 'sweating system' in the manufacture of slop clothing and the cheaper lines of boots, furniture and cigarettes and in women's work generally. Disguise as a tailor-hand allowed Webb to observe labour in a tailor's workshop without impinging on the behaviour of the people she investigated. It also enabled her to become one of those she was observing and thereby transcend the class divisions that usually separated her from the people she investigated. In her work, Webb tried to make clear that such a condition did not exist between alien and English workers, that it existed in places and trades where no foreigners—or Jews—worked and that Jewish workers were confined to only a minority of the 'sweated trades.' The investigator, she writes in *My Apprenticeship:*

> ...surveyed all the industries in which the evil conditions of sweating prevailed, whether in the metropolis or in provinces, the Jewish workers were found to be but a fraction of the whole body of workers and also, to a large extent, a non-competing group, confined to the manufacture of certain commodities, in many instances commodities which had not been produced before. In short, if every foreign Jew resident in England had been sent back to his birthplace, the bulk of the sweated workers would not have been affected, whether for better or for worse.[4]

If 'sweating' was not the result of foreign immigration, neither was it, Webb believed, merely a system or means of organising labour with the use of subcontractors, the subdivision of labour middlemen and certain kinds of machinery. These aspects of trade organisation simply did not define or create the abuse of exploited labourers. Webb worked towards a redefinition of 'sweating'—that it represented 'no particular method of remuneration, no peculiar form of industrial organisation, but certain conditions of employment.'[5] She noted that 'sweated' conditions did not necessarily indicate the existence of low pay and inadequate work facilities.

Booth's and Webb's newly-found anti-individualism did take different forms and led, ultimately, in two very different directions. Booth's 'socialism' was a way of trying to preserve a non-socialist society. Webb's anti-individualist suggestions were both more practical than Booth's and more directly aimed at the problem that had been uncovered at the base of poverty: the conditions of labour.

If the investigation of East End labour convinced Webb of the destructive side of individualism, her experience of Bacup provided her with an illuminating contrast to the misery and anomie of urban working-class life and with ideas for minimising the liabilities of laissez-faire capitalism:

> The contrast between the sweated workers of East London and the Lancashire textile operatives made me realise how the very concentration of wage-earners in the factory, the iron works and the mine had made possible, in their cases, what the sweater's workshop, the independent crafts-man's forge and the out-workers home had evaded, namely, a collective regulation of the conditions of employment.[6]

Webb was schooled in an intellectual tradition that, despite its insistence on laissez-faire politics and economics, enabled her to be receptive to collectivist notions of business and government. By 1912, Webb was ready for a new experiment in political organisation, to abandon, finally, the older parties and the policy of permeation, to wind up the National Committee for the Prevention of Destitution and to create an independent socialist party—the nucleus for which might seem to be the Fabian society. Spencer, the man who dropped Webb as his literary executor after she became publicly allied with the Fabians, himself paved the way for her 'conversion' to Fabianism. Spencer's most important legacy, to Webb and to other individualist-turned-collectivists, was his conviction that society evolved and that, as it evolved, it progressed.

What accounted for this transition from the 'old' liberalism of James Mill to the 'new' liberalism of John Stuart Mill, from an emphasis on Benthamite hedonism to an interest in Comtean 'altruism'? The philosophical radicals wanted to prevent the state from abridging individual rights, while the radicals of the 1880s wanted to involve the state in maintaining those rights. For the individualist, free enterprise was the very source of progress; for the collectivist, it was something that needed to be checked in order that real progress might take place. Webb always held to Spencer's equation of process with progress but, while the equation pointed Spencer in the direction of laissez-faire, it brought Webb to the door of collectivism. Webb came to believe in the validity of State intervention in the lives of individuals because she saw collective action as a way of increasing mutual dependence. Rather than impeding progress towards the perfection of social existence, Webb believed that collectivism would express and accelerate that progress. For Webb, legislation that controlled trade and conditions of labour, that provided citizens with health and education, would be an impetus and not an impediment to social progress, mutual dependence and even greater individuation. Up to 1912, Webb herself played little direct part in the Fabian Society. She lectured for it and wrote a tract; she went to the Fabian Summer school in 1908 and 1909 and was its director in 1910. In 1912, she was prepared to take the Fabian society seriously.

The last enterprise, which the Webbs started before the outbreak of the First World War, turned out to be one of the most solid and enduring experiments in journalism. A new paper was required and that paper turned out to be the *New Statesman*. In founding the *New Statesman*, the Webbs showed remarkable judgement and acumen. What they wanted was a Fabian journal, a journal which would put across Fabian principles and the results of the newly founded Fabian Research Committee, which would promote discussion on the social questions of the day from a Fabian angle and generally carry on the work of permeating opinion. But Webb saw quite clearly that if such a journal were run and published by the Fabian Society itself, it would inevitably be labelled sectarian and start its life in hobbles. The problem was how to secure Fabian support and influence without forfeiting the appearance of independence; and this problem she or Sidney, or both together, solved in a highly characteristic manner. The *New Statesman* was rounded as an independent journal run by an independent company. One of the most important tasks it fulfilled was her scholarly work, chiefly relating to English local government.

Webb was trying hard to make the Labour Party a compact force fighting for socialism, but she was not prepared and could not afford to give her full time to it. She was becoming more and more pessimistic about the political outlook. She did not find the Labour Party inspiring. She was prepared to endure a certain amount of inconvenient and distasteful social functioning in the service of the Labour government.

Brought up with a sense of the 'occupational disease' of London society life, Webb could have got married and settled in a more or less functionless upper class life that is called 'social.' Her account of her struggle against the pressures and temptations of the social environment of her class, to escape such a life ('Dissipation does not suit me, morally or physically') and find a vocation is a classic document of self-criticism and intelligence in a young sensitive woman.

Her attempts to train herself in observation and analysis are rewarding as when she declares the importance of 'literary studies' as the main factor in developing as an individual. It is this profound seriousness which makes her reject her class life of luxuries. The quick intelligence with which she scrutinises the politicians, civil servants, intellectuals, public figures and the others with whom she has to deal is the outcome of hard work for self-improvement, unusual of the upper-class mind.

According to Webb, the attitude of man towards the universe—that is to say, the metaphysical atmosphere—is more difficult to describe because the period was one of rapid transition from one metaphysic to another. The dominant impulse was neither the greed of riches nor the enjoyment of luxurious living, though both these motives were present, but the desire for power. The trueborn saint, whether rich or poor, is an uncommon variety of the human species. There was no censorship whether of talk in the family, the stream of new books and current periodicals or the opinions of the crowd of heterogeneous guests. Such was the attitude of man towards man in the social environment in which Webb was reared. It was the continuous uncertainty as to social status that led to all the ugly methods of entertaining practised by the crowd who wanted 'to get into society.'

Living in a stronghold of capitalism surrounded by the pleasure-grounds of London society, Webb distrusted human personality, whether she observed it at work in her consciousness or in the behaviour of other people. From the flight of emotion away from the service of God to the service of man and from the current faith in the scientific method, Webb drew the inference that the most hopeful form of social service was the craft of a social investigator.

Detailed descriptions of the life and labour of the people in all its various aspects, sensational or scientific, derived from personal observation or statistical calculation, become a characteristic feature of the publications of that period, whether newspapers or magazines, plays or novels, the reports of philanthropic organisations or the proceedings of learned societies. It may be said that this novel concentration of attention on the social condition of the people was due neither to intellectual curiosity nor to the spirit of philanthropy, but rather to a strong sense of panic on account of her own shortcomings in light of the newly enfranchised democracy. 'What had been borne into me during my book studies was my utter ignorance of the manual working class, that is, of four-fifths of my fellow-country-men.'[7] These frank and open observations by Webb show us that she was entirely different from the usual politicians of her days, whose typical thought and behaviour were guided almost exclusively by expediency, even downright hypocrisy.

***

My Apprenticeship as an Autobiography

If we examine Webb's memoir in the context of Victorian autobiographical literature, we can recognise it as a breakthrough in the history of women's writing rather than as an example of a woman's retreat from introspection or personal confession. Webb's was the first British woman's autobiography to take the classic Victorian form of spiritual crisis and conversion. Webb wrote in a genre that tended to describe and expose conflict, because it suited her own experience of internal contradiction. There were inconsistencies in her position as a publicly powerful woman and as a religiously-minded Fabian, and she represented these apparent contradictions in *My Apprenticeship* as related and overlapping phenomena.

As described earlier in Chapter 3, the Victorian age was remarkable for the innumerable autobiographies written during this period. 'History is the essence of innumerable Biographies[1],' wrote Carlyle. Carlyle himself found it appropriate to write an autobiographical fiction to accompany and elucidate his 'clothes philosophy'; John Henry Newman, when accused by Charles Kingsley of lying about his religious faith, responded by writing an autobiography entitled *Apologia*; Darwin sought to amuse himself and educate his children by leaving behind a record of the 'development of my mind and character'; Trollope took the opportunity in his memoirs to confess that his 'first object in taking to literature as a profession' was to make money; and John Stuart Mill revealed to his Victorian audience, albeit posthumously, that as a young man of twenty he had suffered a 'crisis' in his mental history.

The autobiographies of a number of eminent Victorians belong to a secular tradition that evolved out of the confessional writings of the saints and was inaugurated in the nineteenth century by Wordsworth's *Prelude*. The process of Christian conversion and redemption was translated in this modern secularised form into what M H Abrams has called the 'painful process of self-formation, crisis and self-recognition[2].' In the Christian 'theodicy of the private life,' it is Providence that gives meaning to pain and defines experience; in the modern form, it is the individual himself or herself who must, in the very writing of an autobiography, both detect and create life's shape, process and meaning.

By virtue of belonging to the Victorian autobiographical tradition, *My Apprenticeship* describes the shape and pattern of life that is derived not only from Webb's experience and memory, but also from the process of writing itself and from the literary models that were available to her. Webb's actual reckoning with other autobiographical texts is a complex issue, as is the issue of any writer's conscious and unconscious connections to literary tradition. We do know from *My Apprenticeship* that she read John Stuart Mill's *Autobiography*, and from her diary that she read Carlyle's *Sartor Resartus*, Goethe's *Faust* and the *Wilhelm Meister* series, Harriet Martineau's *Autobiography* and George Sand's *Histoire de ma vie*. Webb read all of these works in late adolescence and early adulthood, during a prolonged period of spiritual and psychological crisis.

These texts and the very vocabulary they established for understanding the growth of an individual influenced both the way Webb lived her life and the ways in which she thought about it. A general pattern of de-conversion and subsequent rebirth characterises the genre of autobiography to which *My Apprenticeship* belongs— The autobiographer describes a loss of orthodox faith; a period of crisis, acute despair and dejection, when the old faith is found to be inadequate; a search for new faith to fill the void of unbelief; and rebirth in newfound faith and vocation.

A reading of Mill's *Autobiography* and Ruskin's *Praeterita* can show us how much greater depth Webb's *My Apprenticeship* has. One can believe that Webb is superior to Mill and Ruskin simply because that she could be a labour leader and at the same time an author.

If *Praeterita* were an autobiography like *The Prelude*

of *the Education of Henry Adams*, chiefly concerned with self-discovery and spiritual evolution, this would be a serious defect. But it is not a philosophical or schematic work. Ruskin was by nature an impressionist, whereas Webb was not. This is the side of Ruskin's genius which was particularly sympathetic to Proust and there is ample evidence of it in *Praeterita*. Since childhood, he had been in the habit of staring at things and letting the impression sink in. He was, he tells us, only interested in what was near him, or at least clearly visible and present. *Praeterita* is full of things stared at and Ruskin makes evident the kind of impressions which he found most rewarding. As was natural to a long, steady carpet gazer, he liked them to be intricate and rich.

By 1885, Ruskin realised that the only hope for his sanity lay in avoiding, as far as possible, those topics which brought his mind to the boil. He had raged and prophesied in vain. The world had followed its evil and crazy course and at last he felt powerless to alter it. *Praeterita*, for all its apparent ease and tranquility, is an admission of defeat. In *Praeterita*, Ruskin refers quite candidly to his own lack of affection for other people and the absence of any need for affection from them. The general tone of Ruskin's self-analysis in *Praeterita* is not ironical; but, on the contrary, it is of an uncanny detachment. Ruskin was not capable of warm and steady devotion; but he was intensely susceptible to feminine charm. Was there ever an autobiography in which girls are more vividly remembered? Every girl Ruskin saw, from childhood onwards, was imprinted on his memory with all her particularities and seemingly set down, after sixty years, as freshly as if she had just entered the room. *Praeterita* omits something important in Ruskin's life and this is his conversion from a critic of art to a critic of society. Right at the start, he sets the liberalism, respectability and commercial probity of his parents against the power of that imagination which would be the guiding star of his own life. There was always a strong provocative and combative streak in him. Ruskin was in every way a divided man, a rigid moralist and one of the most gifted of all aesthetes.

The greatness of Ruskin's autobiography has the same source as the greatness of his life and achievement. He could never submit to his parents, nor altogether escape them. He could never believe their teaching and he could never reject it. Ruskin has a way of signalling a deep inner change by a changed attitude to a literary text. In that change of feeling Ruskin encapsulates, with the brevity and precision of a great writer, much of the history of his own life. *Praeterita* was certainly meant to be, and perhaps is, Ruskin's calmest and most balanced book. If he found it difficult, or sometimes impossible, to be mild, he could at least redress one extreme with another.

His autobiography is surely one of the greatest autobiographies and especially because of its power of linking the experiences of childhood with the formation of character and the development of genius. And the deep irony of the whole story is that the consecrated child, nurtured to be a genius, really was a genius; yet the nurturing of him to be one maimed and disabled him. This is the central idea of the whole work, breathing unspoken in every line. It has a tragic grandeur.

Autobiography is a species of personal history—a narrative of events occurring in time. At its simplest, it is a straightforward chronicle that begins at the beginning and proceeds, more or less mechanically, toward the present or whatever moment of termination the author has chosen. And yet the ordering of his experiences into a shape that answers better than mere continuous sequence to his notion of what his life really means is often one of the chief purposes of the autobiographer.

We should not forget that there is one fundamental aspect of the autobiography which makes it very similar to other literary forms ranging from sonnet to historical novel. Reading it intelligently involves two kinds of judgement—judgement of the author's idea in writing and of the formal principle upon which he composed it; and judgement of the degree to which the finished work embodies the idea. In autobiography, one may find minor works which perfectly embody a simple idea of limited interest and major works with obvious faults. Also, as in the study of other literary forms, one cannot rely solely on what the author may have said about it to find the idea and formal principle of the work, useful evidence as that may be. There is only one final court of appeal, the work itself, which may not be identical with the author's intentions. In reading any literary work, we have the right and sometimes the duty to introduce considerations ignored by the author. This is especially true for an autobiography, since the last thing any person—however truthful—learns to treat with perfect fairness is the self.

It may be objected that every readable autobiography, like any other sensible account of events, either displays some continuity or it is nothing; and that is true. But the interesting fact is that, in nineteenth-century autobiography, formal continuity is a principle of philosophic, not merely narrative, coherence. It is in some sense the emblem of the real subject of the work, the gradual evolution of an always-identifiable self. Psychological theory and philosophies of causation provided nineteenth-century writers with theoretical sanction for this view of themselves—a view that finds explicit verbal expression in the autobiographers: concern with the growth and development of the self.

Thus John Stuart Mill proposes as one of the chief values of his *Autobiography* the fact that it notes 'the successive phases' of a 'mind which was always pressing forward' and he tells us very little that does not bear on this subject. He habitually refers to his book as a 'mental history,' the record of his 'mental progress,' his 'mental growth' and 'development.' To his Victorian contemporaries, Mill was the 'saint of rationalism,' a stern but sympathetic champion of agnostic rectitude and measured political reform. Mill's *Autobiography* made the story of his father's decision to educate his eldest son to be another intellectual like himself famous. When he was twelve, Mill began the study of logic, metaphysics and ethics, which was to be the crowning feature of his upbringing. Art had no place in the scheme and religious instruction was rigidly excluded. However, Mill felt the need for the culture of the feelings as well as of the mind. Mill saw for the first time the importance of the spiritual, aesthetic things that his father's rationalism had no room for.

The story of this crisis in his life is told by Mill himself in his *Autobiography*, a posthumously published book of exceptional literary merit and one which continues to be read, for its human interest, even by people who have no special interest in Mill's work as a reformer or philosopher. Mill's mind had been too solidly cast in the eighteenth-century mould. He had come to believe that the imagination was as important as reason and the sensibilities as important as the intellect, but he was never to join the romantics in mistrusting reason or in thinking that the sensibilities were more important than the intellect.

The difficulty about the position Mill took up is that the two philosophies he tried to combine, rationalism and romanticism, were opposed on all the central issues: men of Mill's father's kind believed in science, reason, happiness, liberty, equality, the rights of man and radical political reform; such men as Wordsworth and Carlyle believed in the antithetical principles of religion, metaphysics, feeling, inspiration, transcendental morality, political discipline, hierarchy and the conservation of the established order. So, how could one adopt substantial elements of the two philosophies and at the same time remain consistent? Part of the answer must be that Mill was not always consistent. The failure of his education lay in sacrificing to the 'training of the human being for speculation and action' the cultivation of the 'passive susceptibilities.' What had brought on the crisis was not too much of one kind of education, but too little of another. Whatever the reason, Mill had now reached that depth of depression that Carlyle had named 'The Everlasting No.' 'I had now learnt by experience', Mill writes, 'that the passive susceptibilities needed to be cultivated as well as the active capacities.' Mill could still feel; in some sense, as his biographer Michael St. John Packe suggests, he was now feeling more acutely than ever. The trouble was that what he was feeling was the barrenness of the self.

The experience of ideas was inaccessible and he was only mildly sensitive to those other influences that give pleasure. He had now to stimulate that faint sensitivity. All his thoughts and inclinations, he says, 'turned in an increasing degree toward whatever seemed capable of being instrumental toward that object.' It was to Wordsworth that, at last, Mill turned. It was in the winter of 1822–3 that Mill formed the plan of a little society, to be composed of young men agreeing in fundamental principles—acknowledging Utility as their standard in ethics and politics.

The name which Mill gave to the society which he had

planned was the Utilitarian Society. It was the first time anyone had used the term *Utilitarian*; and it made its way into the language from this humble source.[3] Ambition and desire of distinction. Mill had in abundance; and zeal for what Mill thought the good of mankind was his strongest sentiment, mixing with and colouring all others. He never, indeed, wavered in the conviction that happiness is the best of all rules of conduct and the end of life. He felt that the flaw in his life, must be a flaw in life itself.[4] What made Wordsworth's poems akin to medicine for Mill's state of mind was that they expressed not mere outward beauty but states of feeling, and of thought coloured by feeling, under the excitement of beauty. They seemed to be the very culture of feelings which Mill was in quest of. Mill found the fabric of his originally imbibed opinions giving way in many fresh places.

He never allowed it to fall to pieces, but was incessantly occupied in weaving it anew. When he took in any new idea, Mill could not rest till he had adjusted its relation to his old opinions and ascertained exactly how far its effect ought to extend in modifying or superseding them. He regarded the methods of physical science the proper models for political thought. The French Revolution aroused his utmost enthusiasm and gave him, as it were, a new existence. He ceased to consider representative democracy an absolute principle. According to Mill, no great improvements in mankind were possible until a great deal of change took place in the fundamental constitution of their modes of thought.

Webb's autobiography is much rich in interest than Mill's autobiography. The formative experience of Webb's early life was much more richer. Her childhood was not a suffering restrictive intellectuality as that of Mill. Dr Leavis compares her with George Eliot as 'a gifted and highly intellectual woman.' That she has proved herself remarkably in a field very different from that of imaginative art is our main contention.

Compared to Mill and Ruskin, Webb was much more definitely and ideologically committed to the working class. Her concepts were substantially less abstract than theirs. While her language is one of involvement, theirs is the idiom of contemplation and mentally worked-out preferences. Webb dealt closely with the practical aspects of life, beginning with the problem of classes—it is this which distinguished her work the most from those of the other two. While Mill and Ruskin had much academic learning, Webb's learning was always subordinate to her dominant interests, as described here.

***

A Fascinating Moment in Social History

Webb could tell us about her England what a sociologist, an economist, a journalist and a politician could not say. She was involved in the interest of life and she had perceptions of 'a better life' in the profoundest sense of the term.

The nineteenth-century England of Webb was in many ways similar to our present age in India, as we too are now going through a period of industrialisation. In this way, her work throws great light on our industrial conditions. In a classically representative manner, she provided us some of the most important parts of the intellectual history of the nineteenth century. The description of her family and its antecedents is, we can believe, a representative piece of the nineteenth-century social history of England. In her very brief introduction to *My Apprenticeship,* Webb immediately made the link between the self and the public world. She spoke of a 'continuous debate between an Ego that affirms and an

Ego that denies.' Probably she was unaware, in writing this, how much it shows the traces of a utilitarian background. The religious possibility is invoked less for its own sake than for its possible usefulness as a means to a desired end, which has been perceived instinctively as desirable. Possessed of a rare combination of affection, security and personal independence, she was left to ponder why it was that they were a family who gave orders but did not obey them, and wonder how intelligent people could swallow so many contradictions. She had an unusual appetite for facts and an adventurous spirit.

She read Herbert Spencer and soon saw through the ditchwater sophistries that remain only as a monument to the credulity of many of his contemporaries. It dawned on her, as it had on Mill, that utilitarianism might logically take a collectivist as well as an individualist direction. This is a fascinating moment in social history when a young woman belonging to a high capitalist family—a section of society with its traditional dignities, its disdain, even fierce contempt for inferiors and its intellectual cultivation—meets the low classes—the 'others' of traditional society.

The pertinent question is: was the underlying ethos really the same? Did the East End sweater reveal the concealed drives of the Potters, or was he a mere travesty? Webb was not given to jumping to conclusions; she was very patient in amassing facts. But the facts, as she saw them, inclined her gradually to the view that the high and the low capitalisms really were versions of the same thing. No doubt her father would have shared his daughter's distaste for the sweating tailor; but he would have denied any likeness between the tailor's ethos and his own. And perhaps Webb's own sense of this likeness was only intermittent. She was very affectionate, very anxious to please, a little vain perhaps of her own charm and beauty. Above all, she had an enormously strong sense of facts; and were not the refinement, the liveliness, the exciting variety of the Potter family life facts? How could she deny them their own validity? 'To me,' she says in a revealing passage, 'a million sick have always seemed more worthy of self-sacrificing devotion than the child sick in fever.'[1] Her deep-rooted empiricism extended to religion too. Emotions and needs were facts too. She did not know what she believed, but she did know what she felt. And so, in a world where many respectable people were pretending in public to be more religious than they were, she was in the opposite position. Thus, she could write as part of her diary entry for 12 February 1888:

> ...now I enjoy my life. I have fair health, faith in my own capacity to do the work I believe in and I have regained my old religious feeling, without which life is not worth living to one of my nature.[2]

She sometimes used to describe herself as a 'religious-minded agnostic.' This phrase was and is used vaguely and loosely by numerous journalists for sundry people. In her case, however, it was a rare instance of a phrase being exactly applicable to a person. She was always sympathetic in her judgement of real believers and stern against scoffers and materialists. She was so convinced that effective social work required a religious motive that she was driven to ascribe some hidden religious impulse to her husband, a judgement which may be thought to reveal more about the depth of her affection for him than it does of her shrewdness in the understanding of motives.

Her judgement of her own talents was unusually just; here, too, where most people are subject to fantasies or fears, her admirable sense of fact prevailed: She saw herself, as she was, as above all a professional, a professional researcher and a professional politician and diplomat. She was appalled by the high amateurism of the English elite. She complained that while the standard of natural ability in political life was remarkably high, the standard of acquirements was ludicrously low. 'Who,' she asks, 'would trust the building of a bridge to a man who started with such an infinitesimal knowledge of engineering as Balfour or Gorst have of national education...?'

The distinction between politics and administration, though she no doubt acknowledged it in theory, was not vivid to her. Her constant line of thinking on public affairs seemed to be: *Find the facts, decide what actions will best ameliorate them, then carry out the policy*. But this tendency to over-simplify the political process did not by any means make her inflexible. She was a diplomatic professional. Clearly, she thought hard about her status as a woman in a world of men and a woman who had not in the least been defeminised by hard political work. Sometimes she caught herself playing the feminine, personal note, like an actor, and rebuked herself for it. At others, she worried about differing with colleagues because it is so unpleasant for a woman to be disagreeable. She had realistic judgement of the complex male attitude to such an unexpected woman as herself, a compound of chivalry, attraction, wariness and uneasy respect. Sometimes she ticked herself off for having it all—including a normal woman's interest in clothes. But perhaps, there was at the same time a lingering, unspoken thought that she needed to prove to herself that she was not a battleaxe, a feminist or a discontented spinster, but one whose little differences in her extremely harmonious married life always ended in a 'shower of kisses.' On the whole, her femininity was a practical advantage which she was prepared to use, just as her class and money were, and she used all three for what she perceived to be the public good.

A sense of facts is useless without a sense of proportion; and this, too, she had. This aided her to keep her inner conflicts within bounds. Her wish to benefit the poor and her sense of justice did not produce any liking for them. She felt herself to be farsighted where they were improvident, neat where they were clumsy, rational where they were passionate and sentimental. Her fastidiousness, like everything else about her, is honest and sensible. But the strain of the apparently default contrast between ideal and reality, between what the poor ought to want and what they did want, was obvious.

The fascination of her autobiographical book lies in this: It gives a most valuable study of the complex relation between inner life and outer. While her inner life fuelled her public effectiveness, it remained vague to her; her public life was clear, strong and effective, but to her deepest apprehensions, secondary and shadowy. And they show a woman who was at home everywhere, who knew England and all classes as few did, who could live with the humble and influence the mighty, who was consulted by everyone for being supremely competent and who yet was an outsider, alone, separated in thought from her devoted husband, a spiritual stranger, just as her father had been when she went with him to taste Sunday sermons. But unlike him, she was no detached dilettante.

***

Notes

Introduction

1. Beatrice Webb, *My Apprenticeship* (Cambridge: Cambridge University Press,1979), p. ix.
2. Ibid.
3. Ibid., pp. xiii-xiv.
4. Margaret Cole, *Beatrice Webb* (London: Longmans, Green & Co., 1946), p.15.
5. Beatrice Webb, *My Apprenticeship*, pp. 1-2.
6. Ibid., pp. 40-41.
7. Ibid., p. 15.
8. Ibid., p. 28.
9. Patricia Ann Meyer Spacks, *The Female Imagination* (New York: Avon-Discus, 1976), p. 365.
10. F R Leavis, *Introduction to Mill on Bentham and Coleridge* (London: Chatto & Windus, 1950), p. 18.
11. Ibid., p. 18.
12. Ibid., p. 19.
13. Ibid., p. 26.

Webb's Criticism of Her Class

1. Margaret Cole, *Beatrice Webb* (London: Longmans, Green & Co., 1946), p. 27.
2. Beatrice Webb, *My Apprenticeship* (Cambridge: Cambridge University Press, 1979), p. 203.
3. Ibid., p. 207.
4. Margaret Cole, *Beatrice Webb*, p. 35.
5. Ibid.
6. Ibid., p. 37.
7. Ibid.
8. Beatrice Webb, *My Apprenticeship*, p. 274.
9. Deborah Epstein Nord, *The Apprenticeship of Beatrice Webb* (London: Palgrave Macmillan , 1985), p. 140.
10. Ibid., p. 154.
11. Beatrice Webb, *My Apprenticeship*, p. 159.

Portrait of An Ethos

1. Deborah Epstein Nord, *The Apprenticeship of Beatrice Webb* (London: Palgrave Macmillan, 1985), p. 31.
2. *Letter to Sidney Webb*, November 1891, Passfield Papers, 11.3.11.
3. Deborah Epstein Nord, *The Apprenticeship*, p. 40.
4. Ibid., p. 48.
5. Margaret Cole, *Beatrice Webb* (London: Longmans, Green & Co., 1946), pp. 112–113.
6. Beatrice Webb, *My Apprenticeship* (Cambridge: Cambridge University Press, 1979), p. 39.

Webb's Interest in the Working Class

1. Beatrice Webb, *My Apprenticeship* (Cambridge: Cambridge University Press, 1979), p. 171.
2. Ibid., p. 172.
3. Ibid., pp. 299–300.
4. Ibid., pp. 319–320.
5. Ibid., p. 318.
6. Ibid., pp. 335–336.

My Apprenticeship as an Autobiography

1. Deborah Epstein Nord, *The Apprenticeship of Beatrice Webb* (London: Palgrave Macmillan, 1985), p. 19.
2. M H Abrams, *Natural Supernaturalism: Tradition and Revolution in Romantic Literature* (New York: Norton, 1971), p. 95–96.
3. John Stuart Mill, *Autobiography of John Stuart Mill* (London: Longmans, Green, Reader & Dyer, 1874), p. 79.
4. Ibid., p. 145.

A Fascinating Moment in Social History

1. Beatrice Webb, *My Apprenticeship* (Cambridge: Cambridge University Press, 1979), p. 249.
2. Ibid., p.120.

BIBLIOGRAPHY

Primary Sources

Webb, Beatrice. *My Apprenticeship*. Cambridge: Cambridge University Press, 1979.

Secondary Sources

Abrams, M H. *Natural Supernaturalism: Tradition and Revolution in Romantic Literature. New York: Norton, 1971.*

Cole, Margaret. *Beatrice Webb.* London: Longmans, Green & Co., 1946.

Cole, Margaret. *The Life of G.D.H. Cole.* London: Macmillan, 1971.

Ebenstein, Williams. *Great Political Thinkers*: *Plato to the Present*. New Delhi: Oxford & IBH, 1977.

Letter to Sidney Webb. Passfield Papers, 11.3.11, November 1891.

Nord, Deborah Epstein. *The Apprenticeship of Beatrice Webb*. London: Palgrave Macmillan, 1985.
Leavis, F R, *Introduction to Mill on Bentham and Coleridge*. London: Chatto & Windus, 1950.

Mill, John Stuart. *Autobiography of John Stuart Mill.* London: Longmans, Green, Reader & Dyer, 1874.

Spacks, Patricia Ann Meyer, *The Female Imagination.* New York: Avon-Discus, 1976.

***

Dr T Sumathy (aka) **Thamizhachi Thangapandian** is a trailblazer in Indian politics, literature and academia, seamlessly combining her roles as a parliamentarian, poet, playwright, lyricist, and educator. Currently, she is the Member of Parliament, South Chennai constituency and is a prominent voice advocating progressive values, cultural preservation and social justice. Her dynamic career spans multiple domains, making her an inspiring figure in contemporary India.

Born in Mallankinaru, Virudhunagar district, Tamil Nadu, Dr Thangapandian grew up in a family deeply rooted in public service and education. Her father, the late Thiru V Thangapandian, was a respected leader in the Dravida Munnetra Kazhagam (DMK) party, serving as a Member of the Legislative Assembly and as a Minister for Cooperation and Commercial Tax in Tamil Nadu. Her mother, Thirumathy Rajamani was a teacher. Inspired by her parents' dedication to the welfare of the people, Dr Thangapandian imbibed the values of service and leadership from a young age.

Dr Thangapandian's academic credentials are a testament to her intellectual rigour and passion for literature. She holds a Bachelor's degree in English Literature from Sri Meenakshi College for Women, Madurai Kamaraj University, where she began her exploration of literary traditions. She went on to earn her Master's degree and M Phil in English Literature from Thiagarajar College of Arts & Science, achieving the distinction of being a university rank holder. Her academic journey culminated in a PhD from the University of Madras, with her dissertation titled *Diasporic Longing and the Changing Contours of Resistance in the Plays of Ernest Thalayasingham Macintyre*. Her scholarly work reflects her deep engagement with diasporic studies, post-colonial literature, and themes of migration and identity.

Dr Thangapandian had a distinguished career in academia and has served as a Senior Lecturer in the Department of English at Queen Mary's College, Chennai, from 1996 to 2008, and held teaching positions at Valliammal College for Women and PGP College of Arts & Science. Her academic contributions extended beyond the classroom as she presented papers at numerous national and international conferences, covering topics such as post-colonial literature, Tamil diaspora, and translation studies. Her insights on cultural identity and literary narratives have significantly enriched academic discourses.

As a writer and poet, Dr Thangapandian has carved a unique niche for herself in Tamil literature. The author of 22 books across Tamil and English, her work addresses themes of feminism, environmental consciousness, and cultural heritage. Her poetry, marked by vivid imagery and emotional depth, has been translated into several languages, including English, Hindi, Bengali, and Galician, earning her widespread acclaim and multiple literary awards, including the *Paavendhar Bharathidasan Virudhu* by the Government of Tamil Nadu in 2009. Her books are studied in university syllabi across Tamil Nadu, underscoring her influence on contemporary Tamil literature.

In addition to her literary accomplishments, Dr Thangapandian is an accomplished theatre artist and has performed in numerous plays of Tamil literary icons, including Bharathiyar and Inkulab. Her performances have explored feminist and socio-political themes, showcasing her ability to connect artistic expression with social commentary.

Dr Thangapandian made a seamless transition from academia and the arts to politics, inspired by her family's enduring legacy of public service. She is currently the Deputy President of the Art, Literature, and Rationality Wing and the chief executive committee member. In 2019 and 2024, she won the South Chennai parliamentary seat with a decisive margin, becoming a prominent Woman Parliamentarian in Tamil Nadu.

As an MP, Dr Thangapandian focuses on education, women's empowerment, environmental conservation, and public health and has spearheaded the *Valimai Thamizhachi* project to establish skill development centers for youth employability. Her commitment to gender equality and progressive legislation is evident in parliamentary debates. She is the global and Indian co-chairperson of the Parliamentarians Group for Clean Air and the first Indian parliamentarian to join the Inter-Parliamentarians Coalition to End Plastic Pollution, helmed by French MP Phillippe Bolo.

She is also a member of a standing committee on Women & Child, Education, Youth, and Sports departments and of a consultative committee for the Ministry of Environment and Climate Change.

Dr Thangapandian has also made her mark as a lyricist and dialogue writer in the film industry, having penned the song, *Pogum Paadhai* for the critically acclaimed film, *Pisaasu.* She has written dialogues for the Tamil adaptation of *Queen*, titled *Paris Paris*. Her creative versatility continues to inspire artists and audiences alike.

Her political achievements have been recognised with several honours, including the Tamil Nadu Best Member of Parliament Award (2019–2024) and the 2023 Parliamentarians Group for Children (PGC) award for her work on child rights.

She has also represented India in cultural and literary forums and is a global ambassador for Tamil culture and heritage.

Her multifaceted career exemplifies her commitment to excellence and her unwavering dedication to social justice, cultural preservation, and progressive values. Her journey as a poet, educator, politician, and cultural ambassador is an inspiration to all, embodying the spirit of service and leadership in its truest form.

She can be reached at:

LinkedIn: https://in.linkedin.com/in/thamizhachi-thangapandian-0a09802a7

Facebook: https://www.facebook.com/thamizhachith/

X (formerly Twitter): https://x.com/thamizhachith

Instagram: https://www.instagram.com/__thamizhachi__/?hl=en

Email: contact@ithamizhachi.com

ithamizhachi@sansad.nic.in